Deliver Us from Fear

Deliver Us from Fear

Eileen Guder

Word Books, Publisher

Waco, Texas

Deliver Us from Fear

Unless otherwise credited, all Scripture quotations are from *The New Testament in Modern English* by J. B. Phillips, © 1958, 1960, 1972, by J. B. Phillips, and published by the Macmillan Company.

Quotations marked RSV are from The Revised Standard Version, copyrighted 1946 (renewed 1973), 1956, and © 1971 by the Division of Christian Education of the National Council of the Churches of Christ in the U.S.A., and are used by permission.

The quotation marked NEB is from *The New English Bible,* © The Delegates of The Oxford University Press and The Syndics of The Cambridge University Press, 1961, 1970, and is used by permission.

To
my husband,
William M. Triplett

Contents

—1—

Fear—

Can We Cope with It?

Have you ever been afraid? I'm sure you have—we all have. There's nothing disgraceful about being afraid. It's inevitable and natural for human beings—frail creatures that we are—to be afraid. Jesus wouldn't have said, "Fear not," so many times if he hadn't known how prone we are to fear.

This book is not an attempt to build a case for the idea that we can live without experiencing some degree of fear, from a twinge of anxiety to sudden overwhelming fright.

There is convincing evidence, however, that we were not meant to live in a constant state of apprehension, nor be obsessed by a nameless sense of danger so that we live timid, colorless lives. Of all people, Christians have the right to be confident and sanguine. After all, the phrase, "Fear not," was not a meaningless attempt to make us feel better, but was meant to be taken literally. For us, there is good reason to fear not.

Yet, as I listen to the talk of the average Christian and observe some of our behavior I discover that we are all too often as fearful and timid as those who have no faith at all. I believe we are failing to use the resources we've been given if we are always preoccupied by possible threats to our well-being.

9

I'm not speaking from some Olympian height, as though fear were not at times a part of my life. (There are people like that, just as there are rare individuals who have never had a headache, never been bored or ill. They often have no sympathy for others less fortunate.) The rest of us, the ordinary, sometimes up and sometimes down people, know what it is to be alarmed and uneasy for no apparent reason. We know what it feels like to be consumed by anxiety or nibbled away by worry. We are the ones to whom Jesus offers help. What I will attempt to do is to show what the sources of our fears are, what the available resources are, and how we can take these and make them effective.

I have all the credentials necessary to deal with fear, because as long as I can remember I have been prey to all sorts of anxieties. It may have come from a very early experience when I overheard my parents and an aunt talking about the terrible things that had happened to people they had known. I remember thinking at the time that the world was a very dangerous place. On the other hand, timidity may just be part of my emotional constitution. If unborn children have thoughts at all, mine at the moment before birth must have been, "I won't go, I'm afraid!" I'm sure that with my first breath I exclaimed, "Oh, I know I'm not going to like it here!"

A Realistic Basis for Coping

Becoming less fearful of life in general and learning to cope with specific fears began when I gave myself—along with all my anxieties—to Christ. That was the starting point and the basis upon which every step toward a more confident life was taken. The confidence, of course, had to be in Christ and not in myself. It was not a matter of saying, "Come, now, there's nothing to be afraid of. All I've got to do is to have courage!" The courage just wasn't there.

Instead, and far more realistically, I was learning to trust

Christ, who is everything I am not, and who has promised to be—in me—all that I can never be on my own. I use the word *realistic* because I am convinced that any other grounds for confidence are illusory. It *is* a terrifying world—without him. With him we have reason to be encouraged, and all the help we need to deal with whatever our fears may be.

When Fear Is Necessary

Before we begin to think about the fears which depress, immobilize, and take the color out of life, it must be said that there is a fear from which we ought *not* to be delivered, which is positively beneficial. It is that fear which sends adrenaline boiling into our bodies and impels us into action when sudden danger confronts us. As I am crossing the street and see a car roaring down upon me, my eyes and brain do an instant calculation which tells me it's not going to stop. Fear moves me into action. It's the fuel that propels me out of the way.

When the crisis is over, the fear is gone. It was *about* something immediate and it was necessary. After such experiences we release our heightened emotions by describing what happened and what our feelings were to others, ". . . and when I saw that monster coming right for me and he wasn't braking at all, I made it to the curb in one jump. I was so frightened I could hardly stand up. . . ."

When my daughter Carole Ann was a toddler I looked up from weeding the front lawn to see her starting into the street just as a taxi turned the corner. I will always remember that instant. I remember standing a few seconds later with her in my arms on the sidewalk, but I have no memory of the moments in between, only of terror which dictated my action, the sound of tires squealing and the taxi driver swearing. Fear got me into the street to get Carole Ann and out again in a hurry, and fear slammed that driver's foot on the brakes.

"Seein' Things at Night"

There is a kind of fear, however, which rather than getting us into action, simply gnaws away at our serenity. It is the fear of possible eventualities which seem to be threatening. We may push these worries far back into our mind, even down into the subconscious mind, but an ominous headline in the morning paper or an unexpected pain is enough to bring them surging to the surface.

It doesn't matter whether you are afraid of nuclear war, a world-wide depression, a stock market collapse—or some purely personal disaster—if it's the sort of thing one can do nothing about. Fear of events out of our control is deadly just because there is no action we can take. When we are able to do something we use up the energy that otherwise, having to go someplace, turns back on itself and, like cancer, proliferates horribly. Boilers explode when the steam gets to a certain point, and some of us are so swollen with fear we are at the exploding point.

When I stop to think of all the demonstrations of that anxiety at hand, my mind goes back to a poem my mother used to recite—she used it as a half-sympathetic, half-derisory, counter to my constant fearfulness. It's by Eugene Field, and the person speaking is a little boy in the country:

I ain't afeard uv snakes, or toads, or bugs, or worms, or mice,
An' things 'at girls are skeered uv I think are awful nice!
I'm pretty brave, I guess; an' yet I hate to go to bed
For when I'm tucked up warm an' snug an' when my prayers
    are said,
Mother tells me "Happy dreams!" and takes away the light,
An' leaves me lyin' all alone *an' seein' things at night!*

"Seein' things at night," is an experience we all know first-hand, not to mention the gray wisps of worry that haunt us even in the brightest sunlight.

For some, the spooks rise out of the financial page of the morning newspaper; the possibility of financial disaster is omnipresent and all plans and decisions are taken with a view to its prevention. One man I knew tithed with a kind of grim calculation, convinced that in doing so he was meeting all of God's demands for righteousness, and it was therefore obligatory on God's part to keep him from any financial loss. There are many, many Christians who believe this and if you are one of them your blood pressure is already rising. Before you slam the book shut, stop a moment and think: Do you give because you love to, because having a part in what God is doing in the world is exciting and joyous, or because you are afraid if you don't you'll be punished? Giving *ought* to be out of a full heart, not out of fear—and if fear is part of your giving then you need this book.

On the other hand, there are those whose constant worrying about money prevents them from ever using it with joy at all. Spending has become a grim business; every dollar is laid out with anguish, and only after much trauma on the part of everyone involved. When money becomes so important in the scheme of things that what we do with it— whether we spend it, save it, or invest it—becomes the occasion for tension and quarrels, there is obviously a problem and it is usually fear.

We are also concerned to a high degree with our physical comfort—not just our safety, but our comfort—and that obsessive interest in keeping our bodies in just the right temperature and away from anything hard or wearing or abrasive is related to the money worry. They are first cousins, they both have to do with safety and with the absence of any kind of hardship.

The Last Enemy

Concern with one's bodily well-being leads inevitably to apprehension about illness, or accident, and the final threat

—death. I don't mean a normal shrinking from that experience which is the ultimate mystery, but a dread so overwhelming that it dominates life. A young woman I knew always said she never wanted children, and she said it long before concern about overpopulation made her view widely held. When she married it was with the understanding that there would be no children; she said the world was getting rapidly worse and this was no time to bring more children into such a perilous place. When some years later she discovered that she must have a hysterectomy she said bitterly, "I might as well have gone ahead and had a baby. The chances of dying on the operating table are as bad as the chance of dying in childbirth." Her real fear was that of death.

We can reassure ourselves on other matters by consulting a doctor, an accountant, or possibly a lawyer, but the fear of death is something no man can banish. The Bible is our only word on that. I believe that when we see what it has to say, and all that Jesus said and did, we will be surprised at the magnitude of the deliverance from fear that is available to us. Not only freedom from the fear of death but freedom from fear of life, which is the other side of the dark coin.

Too Scared to Live

If that sounds paradoxical, it is nonetheless true. Those I have known who were inordinately afraid of death ended up by being afraid of living as well. Most of our activities in life involve a certain element of risk. It's a very small step from being afraid of death to being afraid of anything which exposes us to possible harm, which could lead to death.

My children used to play with a little boy in the neighborhood whose mother was so afraid that he would pick up a germ or have an accident that the poor child was never allowed to do anything. He couldn't have a bicycle because he might fall and hurt himself; he couldn't go outdoors if the temperature was a few degrees under normal because he might catch cold. If it was a warm day, he was told anxiously not to run about too much, he might get sunstroke. He was never allowed to eat away from home because his diet was carefully planned and, obviously, his mother didn't think the rest of us fed our children the right way. At the slightest sign of a sniffle, or a lagging appetite, out came the thermometer and an impressive array of medicine bottles.

When there was a gathering of the mothers in the neighborhood, this woman tried to educate the rest of us as to the proper way to raise our children, feed our families, and keep ourselves healthy.

"No thank you," she'd say when offered a cup of coffee, "coffee is very bad for you—it washes the vitamins right out of your body." She and her husband didn't socialize with anyone at all because their early bedtime was about the time most parties started. She read every book on health there was and quoted extensively from all of them.

Unless she derived some enjoyment from all she did in the name of good health, the regimen that dominated every day, there was very little return for all her preoccupation with being safe from all possible threat to life and limb. She was one of the dullest women I've ever met. I can't see that there was any other reward, for she and her family were not particularly healthy. There wasn't anything really wrong— they just all looked a little wan and pasty, and were prone to catch cold easily.

I admit she was an extremist, but not all that unusual. Life, for too many people, seems to consist mostly of trying to make sure that there are no risks. Of course, no one wants to get hurt or be ill, but to live every moment with that kind of fear makes life very bleak.

There is also the fear of being hurt emotionally. Whenever witnesses to a crime explain why they made no attempt to help the victim they usually say, "I just didn't want to get involved." That's the philosophy of a great many people today about life itself, which consists of relationships. They don't want to get involved because they don't want to get hurt. They are possibly the most to be pitied because their fear isolates them more surely than stone walls. It's a very contagious fear, too, at least these people seem to want to infect others. When I began dating after five years of widowhood, a friend called to warn me that I shouldn't allow myself to care for anyone. "I just don't want to see you get hurt, Eileen," she said earnestly. That's the way far too many people feel about relationships—don't get into them if there's the slightest chance of being hurt. That seems to be inconsistent with the Christian life, and certainly with any kind of enjoyment of life.

The Fear That Isolates

There is still another kind of fear which is prevalent in our western culture—the fear of failure. It has its opposite side, too—idolatrous worship of success. I stated earlier that fear often immobilizes, and the fear of failure certainly does. The moment you begin any project you run the risk of possible failure, and one way to make sure that never happens is simply not to do anything.

We're all acquainted with this fear in one of its most uncomplicated forms—the anxiety with which we used to approach a final examination at school. Most of us were able to function pretty well in spite of our nervousness, but a friend of mine always broke out in fever blisters just before an examination. No matter how well prepared she was, no matter how thoroughly she had studied, two or three days before the examination the blisters began to break out. There was a very good reason for her tenseness—her father and mother demanded a perfect performance, and she was never sure she was up to it.

Perhaps that's the case with many of us. Someone—ourself or others whose good opinion we feel we must have—demands a perfect performance and we know we're not capable of it.

· Up to this point we have been discussing fears which are highly individual, some of them so personal we never admit to anyone that they exist. But now we come to different territory. Fear of failure and its opposite, success worship, have spread from our personal lives into the church. The kinds of fear we will discuss from this point on are fears which are particularly evident in the church. They may have their origin in each one of us and our own specific anxieties, but they have come to have a particular shape and form in the Christian community.

Fear of failure can keep a man from leaving a job he dislikes in order to do what he really wants to do, because risk is involved. I knew someone like that and he remained at a job he really loathed because he was afraid that if he got into business for himself he wouldn't make it financially. His wife used to encourage him to make the break but he usually said, "Sure, that's easy for you to say—you don't have to bring in the money to pay all these bills and feed these kids." She told him she'd be willing to get a job. Since the children were all in school she would rather like to work again. At that he always became very huffy and told her he was still capable of supporting his family, and a little more encouragement from her would be better than telling him he wasn't taking care of them. This was so illogical that she tried a few times to convince her husband that it wasn't dissatisfaction with his provision for the family that was her motivation, but rather a desire to help him be free to do what he really wanted. These discussions always ended in an ugly quarrel and a strained relationship which lasted for days, so she finally gave up.

Her husband continued the work he found dull. When he got to talking with other men about work he frequently said, "Well, of course, I've always wanted to get into something for myself. I like fixing things, maybe a small appliance repair business or something, but the wife and kids kind of like money coming in regular." By implication, he handed the responsibility for his reluctance to go into business on his own to his wife and children. She knew the real reason of course. "He's afraid he'll fail, Eileen," she told me once in a moment of rare bitterness, "and he's got to have someone to blame. He's told himself that I'm the one who wants security for so long that by now I guess he really believes it."

That man's fear of failure did something to his whole family. It left a disillusioned wife who regarded her husband with tolerant contempt, two children who went their own way as soon as they were old enough, sure that there must be more enjoyment and excitement to life than they had found at home. Fear does something to everyone it touches. Either it spreads like a disease or, as in this man's family, alienates and isolates its victims from those around them.

The Fear That Distorts

But when fear of failure gets into the church its consequences are devastating because it produces a climate in which our thinking becomes confused and our standards distorted. The fear of failure and worship of success are inevitable when we become afraid of the world and seek to withdraw from it. Since it isn't possible to get completely out of the world (we do have to go to work, get an education, shop, and cannot escape the consequences of political and economic events), we often do the next best thing. We keep our relationships with people and organizations outside the church as nominal as possible and live our real lives totally within the society of Christians.

This is demonstrated by a sentence I've heard from women on so many occasions that when they utter the first words I know what the rest will be. "Yes, we have to belong to the Rotary Club (or the Kiwanis or the Lions Club or the Chamber of Commerce) because of Jack's business. But *of course* we never go to any of their parties. We have nothing in common with them." My conviction is that the attitude of mind that brings forth such a sentence is profoundly unchristian. I believe we were meant to live our lives out in the world where the action is.

Fear Spawns Other Evils

Fear can have a devastating effect on any body of believers when it is allowed to go unchecked. Just as we are of no use to Christ at all when we're afraid to get out in the world, we subvert and corrupt all we are meant to be as a church when we live as a segregated group of people determined to be safe from contamination by the world.

The church that is dominated by a fear of involvement in the world, and has turned in upon itself, shows four major characteristics which are the result of that fear: snobbery, the ghetto attitude (Christian subculture), social climbing within the church social structure, and an inordinate suspicion and fear of other Christian groups whose culture is slightly different. This last characteristic, the suspicion of other Christian groups, is exemplified by two statements that were made to me. One woman, speaking of her college-age daughter, said worriedly, "Of course, she's dating a fellow right now rather steadily, but we hope she won't get too serious. He's a *Lutheran*." Another woman said to some of us in a Bible study group, "When you join a church, be sure it's a Bible believing church, not some liberal Presbyterian bunch." I asked her why and she replied, "Well, you all know what Presbyterians are." Managing to keep my temper, I said, "You'd better tell me. I've been a Presbyterian for years and didn't know there was anything to distinguish us from any other Christians."

The Threatening Face of Change

There is also another fear which is deadly to any real vitality in one's life—or the life of any church—the fear of change. We can be afraid of change for so many reasons. Often the known is less threatening than the unknown. We are more comfortable with what is familiar. We know what to expect, how to react. As we grow older, change of any kind is symbolic of changes in ourselves which we find hard to accept—all the signs of growing old. Though we can't stave them off indefinitely we can avoid facing them if we are able to surround ourselves with the comforting reassurance of an unchanged *milieu*. That is why, when the social structures, including the church, begin to change it is very difficult for us to accept these reminders of our own mortality.

The current wave of nostalgia which is evident in television, motion pictures, music, folk art, and literature, as well as in women's clothing, is an illustration that everyone is uneasy in a world which is changing too rapidly for comfortable adjustment. We long for simpler, less complicated times. They weren't, of course. It's just that in retrospect, frozen in their period of time, we can remember them in tranquillity.

The fear of change which we all experience to some degree as individuals exists in the church because we bring it in with ourselves. Most of us view the transformations that are taking place around us with emotions varying from enthusiasm on the part of younger people to acceptance from most of us to hostility and resistance from a few. But hardly anyone contemplates changes in every segment of society around us with complacency; for many of us these changes appear likely to put an end to a life-style with which we are comfortable.

There is no way to eliminate the consequences of change in our lives, and some of them will be sad; but there is a way to accept, and cope with change gracefully, if not with enthusiasm. We will explore this in more depth later. It may look a little less ominous to us as we think about change to consider some of the inescapable results of trying to keep any part of life safe from its touch. There are some problems inherent in every condition of life, and we may discover that what results when we strive to keep "our group" untouched by change is worse than anything the change itself could bring.

The Fear of Witnessing

Witnessing is a vital part of the Christian life. Indeed, it is not just a part, it is inherent in the life itself. We can't help demonstrating to the world around us what we are, what makes us tick. As fundamental as witnessing is, however, it is also a problem to many of us. We may agree on its necessity, but we disagree on just how it is accomplished.

I believe this disagreement arises primarily out of a misunderstanding of witnessing, or an overemphasis on one of its facets. In my own life I've gone from one to the other of the two major views of witnessing, until it seemed that there must be a truer, more biblical way. One point of view is that it is chiefly a matter of telling others about Christ, and therefore how one goes about that is all that matters. Method becomes everything, a kind of salesmanship. The other way of thinking about witnessing, often arrived at in reaction to the obvious flaws in the first view, is that the way one lives is all there is to it. We are what we do. We show, not tell, our faith.

In my own life I followed an almost classic pattern; adopting the first point of view with all the enthusiasm of a new Christian. Taking all the courses, learning the Bible verses, and then talking to everyone who came within my orbit. I *was* a kind of salesman—not very good. Eventually there was a reaction on my part; I swung widely the other way. The phrases and clichés often used in witnessing became abhorrent to me. I do not believe that was a balanced point of view, nor a healthy way to live the Christian life. I will later attempt to lay out what seems to me to be the middle way—the way we were intended by God to be his witnesses.

Facing and Conquering Fear

Life can be truly exciting when we are really free of crippling fears. Most of us have hardly begun to grasp the magnitude of the freedom that can be ours. We think being free of fear means being safe and protected, that there is no need for anxiety; but that's really not freedom at all. To live like that is to be in bondage to whatever set of circumstances we need to have in order to feel quite safe.

Real freedom from fear is present even when we are in the midst of very dangerous situations, or confronted with sudden disaster or bad news. It's the only kind of freedom from fear that God offers to us, not because he's unwilling to give but because this is the best there is. There are two things it does for us. It frees us from the slow, wearing poison of constant anxiety and apprehension; and it enables us to do and be what we were really intended.

We were meant to be God's agents in the world, not as spectators, observers, or advisers, but as participants. When we haven't been it has usually been out of fear—the fear of getting hurt or being laughed at or simply of being uncomfortable in a strange milieu. But nothing good ever happens in the world unless someone makes it happen, and we are the ones God intends to use. Delivered from the inhibitions and restrictions of fear, we *can* fulfill that task.

First, however, we must call our fears by name, describe them and what they do to us, and then put the remedy to work. It's a little like getting over an illness: first the diagnosis, then the treatment, and finally, freedom!

I was reminded of that recently when my three-year-old granddaughter, Megan, was here for a visit. She was terrified of all the animals, and especially of our large black and silver German shepherd, Mike. No one knew why. I could sympathize with her; she was afraid of even small animals, and Mike was as tall as she was. He has long teeth and what must look to a child like a cavern for a mouth. For a long time she screamed whenever he was in the room, so he spent a great deal of time on the back porch. Then she advanced to the point where she no longer screamed but made a convulsive leap into my arms on his approach, locked her arms around my neck and whimpered, "He scares me."

Just admitting her fear seemed to quiet it somewhat. Eventually Megan grew bold enough to pet Mike—timidly, and ready to fly if he turned toward her too quickly, but she'd come a long way. I don't think she would ever have gotten over her first frantic fear if she'd simply kept screaming and hiding her head every time she saw him. She had to look at him, to see that though the teeth were large and the mouth wide that he wasn't going to swallow her, he was merely panting with enthusiasm. She saw that his exuberant bounds through the house and his waving plume of a tail were signals of good will.

We must do what Megan did—look our fears in the face. Some of them will turn out to be exactly like a big black dog:

menacing in appearance, but on closer examination we will find that the danger was in our own minds. There are other fears far more real. When Christ said, "Fear not," he meant those fears as well as the imaginary ones. Once we face them we will find there is a way to be rid of them, and then we will be really free.

—2—

"Safety First"—
Our Creed?

Before we consider the real risks in the world and how we can cope with them—as well as the fears they engender —we must take a good look at the climate around us. When we do, we will discover that we live in an extraordinarily fearful age which has an overriding preoccupation with *safety*.

"Safety First," is a phrase that has acquired an aura of sanctity almost religious. Perhaps that is because it is associated in our minds with admonitory signs at school crossings and little lectures on safety delivered by the grammar schoolteacher in much the same tone as exhortations to be hardworking and honest. We have come to think of the attitude of mind it promotes as being a virtue, as sterling as the American way of life.

People have always experienced an inner conflict between two opposite impulses—a fascination and desire for adventure; and an equally strong urge toward self-protection and safety. I suppose in most of us one of these tendencies is stronger than the other; and in our safety-oriented culture, caution and security seem to be winning.

25

The Thrill Without the Risk

It is no longer necessary, in order to gratify one's taste for excitement or adventure, to accept the risks that go with a venture. We can experience it all, vicariously, right in the comfort of our own living rooms as the television advertisers assure us. It's almost like having the best of both worlds—the thrill of the chase, the deliciously creepy horror of a crumbling castle complete with vampires, the international settings and savoir-faire of the jet set—and all this in glorious color with snacks and drinks by one's side.

I've discovered how fatally easy it can be to allow television to take the place of active involvement in life. There is so much action, much of it far more violent than I will probably ever experience, that if I'm not careful I can dream away hours, days, months, in the euphoria of television watching. It *does* take time, and if I allow that time to encroach upon other facets of my life—being with friends, working at my writing, taking care of the house—then television has become a substitute for real life. It's a danger I must guard against.

The dream that one can have perfect safety is fostered by the fact that we have been able to do away with a great many dangers which once were accepted as inevitable. Science has eliminated so many diseases and found cures for so many others that it tempts us to believe we can get rid of all sickness. Much has been accomplished in the areas of industrial accidents, in both public and private transportation. This leads us to a comfortable assumption that we can conquer the remaining hazards. One reads constantly of new devices which will make air travel safer, eliminate collisions, and remove all risks from flying.

This is all very comforting. Total security may be just within our reach. Then this shallow assurance is abruptly shattered by the news of an airplane crash, an automobile wreck, or word that a friend has leukemia. We are reminded that human suffering and disaster are still very much with us. At such times we ask, "How can a good God permit such things?" Or, if the illness or financial catastrophe strikes us personally, "Why did this happen to me?"

The Vanishing Pot of Gold

There is no way to be sure of complete financial security, of course. As long as we live in a society where the economy functions freely, money can be both made and lost. Even increasing government controls do not, as we can all see now, guarantee a stable economy. In the past few years quite a few people I know have seen a lifetime's investment on the stock market wiped out; instead of early retirement they're planning to work as long as possible in order to recoup.

Inflation, economic uncertainty, and reports of shortages in grain, oil, and other necessities of life, tend to make the climate somewhat apprehensive. A lot of Christians are just as anxious about the financial future as anyone else, and it's easy to see why. But before we run to cash in our savings and buy gold to put away in safe deposit boxes, stop and think: Are we afraid of being hungry, cold, ragged, and homeless? Or are we afraid of being reduced to a lower standard of living than we now enjoy?

For most of us, it's the latter. True, some of us have lost jobs and gone through grim months looking for something in another field, trying to hang on to house and cars—the fear was real, just as the situation was real. But even so, Was there *real* hunger? Not enough food? I think we'll have to admit that while it's extremely unpleasant to give up luxuries that once seemed necessities, to cut corners and adopt an austerity program better suited to the 1930s, we would still have enough.

The rub is that we have come to feel that the full life, the life we are entitled to, is more than just enough, it is more than just having what we need. It means having all we want.

As long as we live in the world we are going to be part of whatever economic, social, or political situation prevails. There's no way God can shield us from conditions which affect our whole society any more than he can give us special air to breathe or special water to drink. To worry about money is an exercise in futility if it means worrying about what the Federal Reserve will do about interest rates or what the Arab countries will do about oil prices. We can't possibly do anything about either. But if to worry about finances means concern over how my family spends its money and orders its financial priorities, then we can solve that problem with action now.

Money worries, like everything else, usually arrive long before the actual problem rings the front doorbell. We see them coming a long way off and begin to be anxious. But, unlike sudden illness, it's possible to do something about impending financial problems.

We can cut down on the fringe expenditures. We can make the old automobile, refrigerator, washer, and dryer, do. Repairs are cheaper than new appliances. We can stop spending with careless abandon and begin planning for what we want to do most. Isn't that better than to go right on spending and fretting about the consequences?

Once we have done all we can to keep ourselves financially solvent we have exhausted our options. At such times (and all too often not until we are desperate) we turn to the Bible to see what it has to say. We look to the Bible for comfort and usually turn to the passage where Jesus tells us that as the heavenly Father takes care of wild flowers, birds, and field grass, he will take care of us. "So don't worry and don't keep saying, 'What shall we eat, what shall we drink or what shall we wear?' . . . all these things will come to you as a matter of course" (Matt. 6:31,33). The eye leaps to these final words, so helpful, so comforting. But we need to go back to the middle of the passage, which advises us to set our hearts on the kingdom of God—and *then* "all these things . . ."

It seems obvious, not only from that passage but from the whole tenor of the New Testament, that the promises are for those who are *in fact,* not just in words, devoted to the purposes of God on earth. That doesn't mean being a missionary or a minister, it means bringing one's whole life into conformity with the pattern of living advocated by the New Testament. Then we are assured that we can bring all our troubles, including our money problems, to God and be sure that he hears and takes our prayers into account. But even then the Bible is not specific about how he will take care of us, only that he will. It seems to promise freedom from actual want, though not the fulfilling of all our desires.

But then, our desires might be radically altered if we were to have our hearts set on the kingdom of God. We so often have them set on other goals, and there is no word of reassurance for these in the Bible. However, if the goals we have set up for ourselves are legitimate objectives and have a place for good in our lives and in the world, then they fit into the larger goal which *is* the kingdom of God, and I believe we can pursue them with a clear conscience. We can pray about them, too, knowing that God cares about us and what we care about. If it is a college education for our children, a farm in the country, a business of our own—it's a legitimate subject for prayer.

That prayer always assumes that we are taking realistic steps toward meeting those goals, not simply waiting for God to hand them out of heaven. I believe that God will help us to overcome our fears about money, no matter how grim the economic picture is, but only if we are living realistically within our financial limits. After all, he is God, not Santa Claus. There are those who regard God sometimes as Santa Claus and sometimes as a vindictive tyrant.

I knew a businessman who spent his whole life building up financial security for himself and his family. When anything, however minor, disturbed his plan he said, "Everything happens to me!" It didn't, of course, but he was so consumed by the desire to be safe from poverty that the slightest setback seemed a financial disaster. He wasn't very different from most of us—we spend a large part of our lives trying to make sure we won't be hurt in some way.

Is This Pain Necessary?

Some of us are more fearful than others. Part of it is native temperament and the rest is environmental influences. I remember how, as a very small girl, I realized that the world was a very dangerous place. Exciting, enticing, yes, but dangerous. I wanted all the adventure and excitement without the danger, if possible. Every night after going to bed I pulled the covers up around my head and said my prayers. They went something like this: "Heavenly Father, please keep us safe from all harm tonight. Especially from burglars, and from fire, and from anything horrible like a gas explosion. In Jesus' name. Amen."

No, that is not an exaggeration. Those were the worst catastrophes I could think of at the time. Later on there were others. Growing up was a matter of discovering that as well as new adventures, new knowledge, new experiences, there were new dangers. One could get hurt so many ways!

We all feel somewhat the same reluctance to accept even the pain one must endure in order to be safe. The discomfort and risk of surgery, for example, may be the only way of avoiding a far worse danger. The pain of having a splinter pulled out and the wound thoroughly disinfected is better than the eventual pain of a festering sore or blood poisoning, but we still dread it. The most common example of all leaps to mind. Few people really like going to the dentist, but we all go. Better the brief pain of the drill than having a tooth pulled.

We are not the first generation to loathe pain and strive for security. But we may be the first generation to *expect* life to be, for the most part, untroubled by discomfort of any kind. Our blind faith in what science can do has brought us to the place where we feel more than just fear when danger of trouble looms, we feel ill-used. And the fear which rises in the throat when we are threatened has in it an element of petulance—this should not be happening to me!

The supreme irony of our situation may be that all our obsession with safety and freedom from pain is combined with a widespread fear on the part of all of us. In the midst of a very comfortable culture, with more medical help than we've ever had, we seem to be threatened by greater disasters than ever, from senseless shootings and bombings, hijackings, sudden undeclared wars, and, ultimately, the cloud of atomic warfare.

The closer we get to making life really ideal the closer we get to large-scale catastrophes. The two opposite facts with which we all live—our very comfortable existence, and the threat of having it suddenly altered by events beyond our control—make for a rather neurotic view of life.

It is in this culture, with its great advantages and its enormous threats, with the ambivalence such an existence produces, that we find ourselves as Christians. We have to come to terms with this world, as well as with our faith, in order to live any kind of life at all, much less with the style our faith demands.

Because it is not possible to be unaffected by the attitudes, the mind-sets, of those around us, we bring them into the church with us. Part of the process of growing as a Christian consists of stripping away the excess baggage that we bring to our faith—the ideas, notions, and prejudices of the non-Christian world.

In a Bible study group one time a friend said, "I seem to be continually discovering not how little I know about the Bible, but rather how wrongly I know it. I've been reading my own ideas into it for such a long time that it's hard to see the words without my own interpretation."

God's Teachers' Pets?

One of these glosses which we read into the Christian faith is our old grammar school idea that safety is a virtue. If it's a virtue, we assume that God must be as interested in making us safe as he is in making us good. Thus we come to equate the ultimate safety Christ promises us with a blanket guarantee to keep us free from trouble in this life.

"I cannot believe that God ever meant for a Christian to be sick," a man once said to me. "I know death comes to us all, but as I read the Bible I see not only Jesus' healing of the sick while he was on earth, but all the promises that if we really trust him, our prayers will be answered."

Another man gave this testimony, "The Bible says that the man who is faithful in tithing will be rewarded—materially. I have found that to be true in my own life, and if any of you will put God to the test you will discover that he does reward the man who honors him."

"I've prayed about my relationship with Bob," a young woman said to me, "and I know that he is the man God has for me. I have the assurance that this is right."

These statements all have one common element—they were made, in all sincerity, by people who believed what they were saying—and every one was proven wrong in that particular case. The man who believed that faithful, trusting Christians would be miraculously healed died of cancer. The man who spoke with such assurance about tithing died broke and in debt. The girl who was sure God had given her the green light on her marriage was divorced three years later.

God Does Care for Us

Why? Were they all fools for believing? Doesn't God offer any assurance of his concern, his guidance for our lives? Or is the problem that each one of these people built a whole Christian viewpoint on a partial truth? We will discuss these issues, and others related to them in later chapters. But here and now is the place to establish the fact that *God does care about us and that when we pray he hears and answers*. Indeed, he hears our prayers better than we pray them: "For example, we do not know how to pray worthily as sons of God, but his Spirit within us is actually praying for us in those agonizing longings which never find words. And God who knows the heart's secrets understands, of course, the Spirit's intention as he prays for those who love God," wrote Paul to the Romans (8:26–27).

The Bible is full of assurances that God is interested in us. Furthermore, his interest is not canceled by our failure to be what we ought to be. He may not be pleased with us, but he never deserts us. All through the Old Testament we see God leading, correcting, but never abandoning his people. Century after century he works with them: the patriarchs, the judges, the prophets.

But We Must Respond

In the writings of the prophets two concepts are tied together constantly: God is righteous and he acts in our behalf

—our proper response is to live in faithful obedience. Right behavior is demanded of the Israelites as being the only proper offering to a holy God who has done something for them—something concrete, something that happens again and again in history.

The Ten Commandments are prefaced by the words, "I am the Lord your God, who brought you out of the land of Egypt, and of the house of bondage" (Exod. 20:2, rsv). God showed his concern for them by his acts. They, in return, were expected to show their gratitude by obedience to his laws.

In the same way, their future welfare was linked to the adherence to the laws God gave through Moses: "If you walk in my statutes and observe my commandments and do them, then I will give you your rains in their season, and the land shall yield its increase, and the trees of the field shall yield their fruit . . ." (Lev. 26:3-4, rsv).

The reverse is also true: "But if you will not hearken to me, and will not do all these commandments, . . . but break my covenant, I will do this to you: I will appoint over you sudden terror, consumption, and fever that waste the eyes and cause life to pine away" (Lev. 26:14-16, rsv).

That was not the final word, however; repentance and reformation would bring help, God would never totally abandon them. All through history the Jews clung to those two promises: that righteous living would be rewarded, and that when they sinned and repented that God would deliver them from their enemies. True, they tended to confuse righteous living with performance of religious observance. They always seemed to remember the finicky details of the ceremonial law more than they did the equally detailed instructions of good behavior. And their history was certainly one of ups and downs which they saw to be the result of their own failure to live according to the laws of God.

Assurance in a Mixed-up World

However, we cannot take these ancient words and simply apply them to the twentieth century, as if they were spoken to each one of us. We look back at the Old Testament from our own viewpoint, which is highly individualistic and subjective. We think about ourselves as single units. The Hebrews thought collectively, not individually. All the promises of well-being for the Israelites were given to the nation, not to individuals. They had their battle casualties, their sicknesses, and their troubles. In Leviticus there are specific instructions for taking care of the poor; there was no all-inclusive guarantee of good fortune for every faithful Israelite.

In actual fact, the same promises God gave the Israelites, he gave his church—even a more staggering guarantee: "the gates of hell shall not prevail against it" (Matt. 16:18, KJV). Along with the inevitability of the triumph of God's people are warnings that we are involved in no sham battle. In the parable of the sower Christ told of the man who is like seed sown on rocky patches—he hears the gospel with enthusiasm but when trouble or persecution arises he gives up his faith. The Sermon on the Mount does not seem to be designed for an ideal world. Jesus advises us to love not only our neighbors, but our enemies who persecute us.

All through the New Testament we find assurances of God's love, care, and the triumph over defeat. Alongside these, however, we find warnings of troubles to come and hardships to be endured. I remember my own confusion as a high school girl reading Matthew 7:7–8: "Ask and it will be given to you. Search and you will find. Knock and the door will be opened for you. The one who asks will always receive; the one who is searching will always find, and the door is opened to the man who knocks."

It seemed to me then that here was an unqualified statement that whatever I asked of God, he would give. Since I was asking for a good many things I never did get, I was not only confused but annoyed. What was wrong? Why didn't God do what the words plainly said he would do? Despite the explanations of pastors and teachers, I fretted over this seeming contradiction for years. It was a long time before I realized that Jesus was talking to people deeply interested in making themselves fit for heaven; and that he illustrated the passage just quoted with a little story about fatherhood—that when a child asked for bread his father doesn't give him a stone, and that God, who is far above the best of earthly fathers, will certainly give good things to them who ask him.

Growing Up to Reality

Perhaps illumination finally came when I could look back and see that most of what I had asked God for would not have qualified as "good things" at all. In my ignorance and short-sightedness I had thought they were; most of those petitions, had they been granted, would have been a disaster. I *was* given "good things," though at the time I was so busy looking for something else that I failed to see them.

That may not sound too satisfactory to someone praying for healing, or for the salvation of a rebellious son or daughter. It is at exactly this point, the point of puzzlement, frustration, and disappointment, that we either grow up or sink back into spiritual babyhood. Babies see life in a very limited way—their little world is all there is. The important figures are those who love them and take care of their needs. For me, growing up was largely a matter of learning more of the world outside my own orbit, and of accepting the wants and needs (sometimes conflicting with my own) of others. I'm still at it.

Christians who never arrive at the point of seeing the

larger picture of life, the vast scope of what God is doing in the world, are like infants who burst into tears at the slightest frustration. Of course it hurts to grow up. All learning is painful. But not growing up, either physically or spiritually, is tragic. It may seem odd that I haven't mentioned faith, nor pointed out the necessity for trusting God in spite of circumstances. It seems to me that faith is conditioned by one's spiritual age. There is a kind of baby's faith—like that of the man who was so sure that tithing brought inevitable prosperity, or the girl who "just knew" that God had told her to marry a particular young man. Their faith was inordinate and it's no use saying, "Well, it wasn't really faith, because . . ." and then qualifying the word *faith.*

Rather it seems to me that God wants us to mature as whole persons. Our faith as well as our emotions and intellect needs to grow up. We need to mature from a faith that is, "Daddy will give it to me if I ask, because I'm his favorite," to "I can trust my Father (though I don't understand what he is doing) because I know him."

Fear is paralyzing. Fear can turn our bones to water and I do not believe we must simply give in to it. The first thing to do is to begin the growing-up process spiritually. We can't begin to cope with fear until we get out of our baby-sized world and look around at what God is doing, and see the largeness of his world and the infinite variety of his people. The Bible has something to say to our fears and we need to look at it seriously; not just the comforting verses which seem to tell us what we want to know, but the whole of it. I believe that when we do, we'll find a far larger reassurance than small comforts for small hurts.

—3—

Neither
Death nor Life

What does the Bible say about some of the specific fears to which we are most prone? Death, for instance: "There are many rooms in my Father's House . . . I am coming again to welcome you into my own home, so that you may be where I am" (John 14:2–3). These words of Jesus were spoken to his downhearted disciples on the night before his crucifixion. If his followers remembered them at all as they huddled in small, disconsolate groups after his burial, then the words must have echoed mockingly in their ears. Not one, but several appearances of Jesus whole and well—different and yet the same—convinced them that he really had overcome death. The astounding resilience and deep joy which marked every member of that first generation of Christians were the result of having been given incontrovertible evidence that the last enemy—death—had been beaten.

There is never any hint, however, in any of Jesus' words or Paul's writings that the fear we all feel about death is sheer nonsense. It would be less than human not to shrink from death because we are aware instinctively that it is frightening as well as mysterious. There is something horrifying about the abrupt separation of one person into two parts—an inanimate body and a spirit with which we can no longer communicate. The mystery lies in the fact that, at death, the person himself—his personality, his singularity—are gone and what is left is empty. The body is no longer the person.

We can overcome that natural fear and horror of death only because of the resurrection. Because of it death is no longer final, a door that slams shut on all our hopes and longings. Jesus went through the door and came back to tell us the other side is better than we would have imagined. But there is no pretense that death doesn't really matter, no sentimental bilge about its being as natural as birth. There are far too many natural facts of life which are painful and frightening. There's none of the shallow hopelessness expressed by non-Christians when they must say something at the funeral: "Well, dear, we must just trust that it's all for the best." The only reason for trusting that all is for the best is a very robust faith in God; and the resurrection is our basis for that faith.

I've heard teachers and ministers say that Jesus wept at the tomb of Lazarus because of his sorrow at the grief of Mary and Martha—they should have known that death had simply ushered their brother into a greater life. I never believed that. I think Jesus wept because he shared their anguish. He, far more than any of us, hated death and until his eventual victory it would be an enemy to be conquered. "Christ, in the days when he was a man on earth, appealed to the one who could save him from death in desperate prayer and the agony of tears," we read in the letter to Hebrews. "His prayers were heard; he was freed from his shrinking from death but, Son though he was, he had to prove the meaning of obedience through all that he suffered" (Heb. 5:7–8).

When Comfort Is Cold

Some Christians, thinking no doubt to be super spiritual, do immeasurable damage to their friends by ignoring the biblical view of death as a real, serious, and dreaded experience which is overcome only by faith in Christ. They offer a cheap, shallow comfort which is no comfort at all. When one is heartbroken at losing someone very dear, what is needed is the assurance that others care and are in sympathy. That is why Paul advised the Christians at Rome, "Share the happiness of those who are happy, and the sorrow of those who are sad" (Rom. 12:15). If he were speaking today he might say, "Please be sensitive to one another. Don't wound someone who is suffering already by pelting him with Bible verses or facile little homilies, but share his sorrow. He needs most to know someone else cares how he feels."

Our two small daughters were in the hospital with polio during that dreadful epidemic in 1948 and the threat of death was very real. We, like many other parents, were consumed with anxiety for our children and clinging somewhat blindly to our faith. One friend made life much harder for me. That was not her intention, quite the opposite. She called me at least once a day to read me Bible verses she thought might be helpful and to give me little homilies on faith and serenity in the face of adversity. I already knew those Bible verses. I knew everything she was telling me was true. But her well-meant advice really hurt; it emphasized the fact that she was *outside* my troubles, looking on, not sharing. What I really wanted was to know that she cared about me and about my daughters.

Years later when a young friend lost his wife he was besieged by the same sort of pseudo-Christian comfort. I say that deliberately, because although quoting Bible verses and uttering platitudes about faith seem to be accepted Christian behavior, when it is done without sensitivity or regard for the state of mind of the recipient it is vain. My young friend, stunned by the loss of his wife and further hurt by being lectured on the meaning of death, was finally met with understanding and genuine comfort when a pastor came and sat down, put an arm around him, and wept with him.

We Are Not Alone

When we are hurt we do not need to have the theology of it explained to us, but to know we are not alone. We know, though sometimes merely academically, that Christ cares about us, about our feelings, our sorrows, and small anxieties. That knowledge is reinforced and changed from intellectual to experiential faith when Christians demonstrate the same sort of caring.

The remarkable grace of God is shown over and over again in the lives of Christians when the time comes that we are faced with death. I believe that Paul's experience in a time of great need is that of most Christians: "My grace is enough for you; for where there is weakness, my power is shown the more completely" (2 Cor. 12:19).

But we need help not only when the crisis comes, but help for us now when we are low-spirited and fearful of death even though it is nothing more than an imagined phantom. We need to be free of fear not only when death is imminent but when it is a nightmare. We must accept, within our Christian perspective, a philosophy of death. We can handle these natural fears of death or separation by accepting the fact that death and separation are inevitable. Nothing is to be gained by looking through the Bible for verses which seem to promise that if we just pray hard enough, long enough, or with enough fervor, that we can ward off its coming.

All men die eventually. Some die sooner than others. A

few years ago I was wakened by a phone call which told me of the tragic death of a young bride. She had been married exactly eight weeks and was killed in an automobile crash in which her husband was totally blameless and the other driver unforgivably careless—an avoidable, stupid, senseless accident. She and her husband were nearly a fairy-tale prince and princess. He was handsome, intelligent, a fine Christian, and she was one of those rare women whose sweetness was genuine all the way through. Their lives were given to Christ in wholehearted service, and they had a great deal to offer the world. Later that morning when I told a young woman engaged to be married what had happened, her reaction was, "How horrible! How can any of us be sure we will be able to marry and have a life together?"

The question is natural, and we all have to deal with it. We aren't the first ones. The Psalms are full of complaints about the difficulties of life which beset the righteous. The conclusion they come to is that our hope is in the character of God himself; and we know more about that than they did, for we have the assurances given us by Jesus and the evidence of his love for us.

God Cares about Our Hurts

That evidence is conclusive. The very fact that Christ became a man, involving himself in life here on earth, sharing our human nature and knowing our limitations and temptations, is an assurance of his deep concern for us. He never turned away sick people by telling them to look forward to heaven, or that they ought to be more concerned with the state of their souls than with their bodies. Whoever asked for help got it.

Of course, he pointed to a healing beyond the physical. He said that man doesn't live by bread alone, that there is a spiritual food and drink far more important than what feeds us physically. But he never implied that physical needs weren't important, or that this life wasn't to be lived fully.

You can't miss the point that God cares about what hurts us, whether we are well or sick, full or hungry, happy or unhappy. If we don't like disease and suffering, how much more must God, who created the world and saw that it was "very good."

His way of coping with the problems of death and disease is not to abolish them by a sweeping miracle. That would still leave the central problem unsolved—the harm men do to each other and themselves by flouting God. Jesus put the problem in perspective. He demonstrated his concern for the daily lives we all live and commissioned his followers to do the same. The parable of the sheep and the goats in Matthew 25 is an illustration of that.

When Faith Becomes Personal

He kept reminding us, however, that what we do here, and the problems we face, signify something more. How we handle illness and death demonstrates our real attitude toward God. We are supposed to do everything we can to get rid of illness, as well as every kind of threat to human well-being.

The Old Testament prophets had a great deal to say about social justice—taking care of the poor, feeding the hungry, helping widows and orphans, and maintaining a strict honesty in business. Jesus demonstrated God's concern for our lives by healing the sick and feeding those who were without food. The New Testament is full of commands to follow that pattern of active caring for the needs of others. Still, sickness, accident, and death are hazards of life. The question is, can they defeat us?

But when we ourselves, or those we love, are struck down,

the issue becomes very sharp: do we trust God rather than circumstances?

When Carole Ann, our oldest daughter, died in 1951 just before her tenth birthday I discovered that God was still there. I did not know why we had to lose Carole Ann, other than the ugly physical fact of a brain tumor. What I needed was to know that what I had believed about God and his love for us had meaning big enough to include—and somehow triumph over—the fact of Carole Ann's death. There were many battles fought silently within me, times I reproached God, accused him of not caring, and finally wept. But when the battles were over the faith was still there, battered but very real. I discovered that faith is merely academic unless it is called into operation, and the times it is needed is when things aren't going well.

At other times, when the problems I was considering were not my own problems but hypothetical postulations, I could intellectualize or spiritualize the problem and work out elaborate systems to explain why things were the way they were. When the problem became personal, however, when it was not "Why does death exist?" but "Why must my daughter die?" both the question and the answer became real. Faith was the means by which the answer came, and it comes into its own when there is no human resource upon which we can draw. We either believe God or give it all up.

But even then it is God who is the ultimate reality. I don't think for one moment that my faith was big enough or strong enough to answer the questions I was asking about death, life, and eternity. Even the faith that I had, and that I have now, came from God. There is no way in which I can explain, or demonstrate, the truth of that statement, except by the way I live.

That last comment will always sound, to non-Christians,

like an evasion. "You talk about your faith," a man said once, "and say your faith comes from God. Well, if there is a God, I don't want that kind of faith from him. I don't want some kind of never-never hope that I'm eventually going to be all right sitting on a cloud somewhere. I want my family to stay healthy and I want to make enough money to get them some of the good things in life." And that is an honest avowal of what most of us want—for everything to be all right.

But when death touches us closely we are forced to consider the fact that no matter how good this life is, it doesn't last forever. *Real* good—permanent good—has to be beyond death. And that is exactly what Christ offers us—permanent good, with no losses, no tears, no clouding of our relationship with him.

The ability to look at death without horror is only because we know that God has given us life. What seems to be the final end to human experience is, for us, only an incident in life. That kind of faith isn't whipped up to get us through sorrows, it comes to us from God. It is the result of putting our trust, however small it may be, in Christ. He does the rest.

Prayer Is Being Honest with God

We are told to pray about everything—not only the enormous shadows that sometimes loom, but about small, even trivial problems. Some people find that comment contradictory. If we can't be sure that our prayers for healing, for health and well-being, are going to be answered the way we want, then why bother? That's exactly the way I felt when I became convinced after reading and rereading the Bible that there was no guarantee of safety in it. Oh, there were assurances of my ultimate safety, all right. But for *now*, for the things I was afraid of in this life, none. Only repeated promises that I wouldn't be alone, Christ would be with me.

That's a grand assurance, but there were many times when I felt like the little girl who was told not to be afraid of the dark because Christ would be with her: "But I want someone with skin on his face!" I wanted something tangible, not some spiritual blessing which, it seemed, could come linked to terribly distressing events. Why pray for something I want, something good for me now if I am going to be given instead some dubious blessing like fortitude, or patience, or faith?

I didn't understand it (and I doubt if anyone ever comes to a complete understanding), but I prayed because Christ told us to. There was that parable Jesus told of the widow who kept bothering the dishonest magistrate until he finally saw that her complaint was taken care of, simply because he was tired of being annoyed by her constant supplications. Jesus pointed out that if a mere man, and a crooked one at that, would act on behalf of a poor woman simply to save himself trouble, then God, who does care for us, would certainly act on our behalf.

The picture I get as I read the New Testament is that God cares so much about our lives that we can come to him with everything, not just spiritual petitions. He knows our tiny worries and petty fears, anyway, so we might as well tell him. We can bring our whole selves to him, freely, without fear of condemnation. That means we can pray about our finances, our health, our families, our frustrations, and our fear of death—nothing is barred.

The important thing is that we communicate our real feelings to God. When we do that he can get through to us with help. That help may be in the form of an answer to prayer which comes just as we had asked. At such times we say that our prayers have been answered. But *all* prayers are answered, that is the character of God. The help he gives may come in the form of fortitude and grace to get through a difficult time. That was the answer given to me when Carole Ann died.

That was my first real glimpse of what eternity is. Our hope is that what we do here, and those we love here, will have permanence. That permanence goes beyond this life. The real meaning of our lives is found in a relationship with Christ and in a future with him. We easily forget it, especially when everything is going well. It is only when part of our happiness is threatened, or taken away, that we come to terms with the temporary quality our lives have, apart from Christ.

The View from the Top

We tend to put our trust in God's goodness in immediate and palpable evidences of it—health, prosperity, contented and successful lives, children who bring us credit—all good things, but no basis for faith. Only when our faith is in Christ and our hope is in life eternal can we live this present life with freedom. Death is a reminder that our lives go far beyond time.

Many Christians, however, seem to feel that to talk about eternity (heaven) is to indulge in spiritual daydreaming. "There's so much that needs to be done right here on earth," they are fond of saying. "We've been accused of dreaming of pie in the sky too long. Let's keep our attention right here where we can do something for God."

It's certainly true that we need to be busy right now, in our present circumstances; but I don't believe that looking forward to heaven is an evasion of duties here at all. Quite the opposite, I am convinced that only when we have a very sturdy hope of heaven can we really handle what we have to do here on earth. When we put our faith in anything we have right now, whatever it is and however good it is, we are trusting in the wrong thing—what Christ *gives* instead of himself. We are also looking at life from too small a perspective, and when events become ominous, or circumstances unfavorable, we get rattled. Life seems to fall in on us.

But the troubles which seem so insurmountable when we feel we have to have everything just right, shrink to their proper proportions when we view them from the perspective of eternity. We can see more clearly and act better from that vantage point. And not only that, but once we have looked beyond death we can better evaluate everything this side of death.

Afraid of Living

Just as some are haunted by a fear of death, others are paralyzed by a similar, perhaps more dreadful, fear of life. The two are very much alike. Perhaps they are even the same. It is certain that for every prick or pain that seems to warn of death there are a hundred frightening possibilities in life. If we draw back from all of them, we'll end up not living at all. Being afraid of all the risks in life ends up in complete paralysis, and it doesn't matter whether one is afraid for himself or for others.

There are many fears in life which may inconvenience us from time to time, or cast a pall over our spirits. But fear of life itself is a fatal disease which reduces its victims to such pallid impotence that they might as well be dead. This fear has one outstanding characteristic (it may masquerade as something else) but at the bottom it is a fear of being hurt by others. When it appears in masked form its captives always say, "I just don't want to get involved," or, "I'm too busy," or, "Men/women are no damned good," or "You can't trust anyone any more."

No doubt in most cases the fear of being hurt arises out of early experiences in life: a mother who rejected, a friend who betrayed, sometimes a group of people who kept one out. I doubt if anyone grows up without having suffered some hurt or rejection. The scars may be small, but they are inevitable. When, for whatever reason, the result is a determination never again to be vulnerable, life becomes colorless. The only really safe place is the grave.

A friend used to worry about her mother. She was so consumed with resentment toward those who had hurt her that she narrowed her circle of friends until there were none left. She was full of long, bitter stories of how she had been neglected, slandered, put upon and generally misused; and she expected her daughter to listen and commiserate. No matter how much she was encouraged to go places where she might make friends—church, club meetings, organizations, etc.—she always said, "No, thanks, I've had it with putting myself out for people. They never appreciate it, they're all just out for themselves. I don't need anyone. My daughter is all I have and all I need."

When her daughter began to date her fury was intense, she felt betrayed. The one person she wanted to keep in her locked-in world was breaking out and she couldn't stand it. In the end, more bitter than ever, she was finally alone. There was no one in her life any more to hurt her, but her life itself was a dead thing.

I've never known anyone to be happy after shutting out the possibility of being hurt in a relationship. It seems to be a law of life that risk is necessary. The only way to avoid it, total isolation, is the sure way to spiritual deadness. We can't live and be close to other people without letting them into our lives, and once we do that we are vulnerable to hurt. But then, so are they.

We easily forget that if we've been hurt, we've also dealt our share of blows. No one is ever the entirely innocent victim. I've noticed that those who are most fearful of getting hurt, who avoid giving themselves in any relationship at all, can be devastatingly cruel in their efforts to protect themselves. They don't seem even to be aware of what they do to others. No doubt that is because total absorption in one's own self leaves no room for awareness of anyone else.

When an individual is so terrified of what others may do to him emotionally that he locks himself in, he is really existing in living death. He will be safe, perhaps, from the ordinary knocks and blows we all sustain, but in a deeper sense he will be in danger of losing his own soul. If one can't give himself to those about him, even those closest, how can he possibly give himself to Christ?

There are two steps that can be taken in order to break out of the self-imposed prison of isolation. First of all one must thank God for his love and acceptance. At first it may be a matter of uttering words and phrases totally opposite to what one is feeling inside. Old habits of resentment, looking for opportunities for grievance, and the accompanying self-pity are hard to break. In my own life I find that allowing resentment toward others to continue usually leads to a whining pique toward God.

But our faith is rooted not in our feelings, which are notoriously variable and undependable, affected by everything from the state of the weather to an upset stomach, but in the concrete actions of God in Christ. We have a dependable record of those actions in the Bible. Reading and rereading the Bible is necessary not only to gain new insights into his will for our lives, but to remind ourselves of what he has already done for us. Thanking him for loving us, for saving us, for his never-failing concern and care whether we feel like it or not is simply banking on what we know to be true— not what we may feel at the moment.

What we are doing when we pray that way is to push out the old, sick negative habits of thinking and feeling with the positive good that comes with spiritual and emotional health. Quite often the sullen, resentful person who hangs back from any kind of commitment to others does so out of a deep sense of inadequacy. He feels he's really not very lovable, so he suspects everyone of rejecting him. I know that in talking about such areas of life I am trespassing on the province of the psychologist. But I believe that many of us who suffer from resentment or a sense of unworthiness can do something positive to get out of our self-imposed prison; and that taking steps on our own toward God may well save us from descending so far into helplessness that we finally have to have professional help.

Anyone can pray. The motivation may be entirely selfish —a desperate sense of loneliness and frustration, perhaps; but that doesn't matter. God, having been gracious enough to come to us in Christ, is no stickler for purity of motive. However we come to him, it is the coming that is important. However childish and selfish our prayers are at first, it is praying that is important. And when we thank him, whenever we turn our minds to his acceptance of us, a little bit of light can come in.

There is a further step to take. As we pray, thanking God for loving and accepting us, we also must begin to pray for others. It's best to pray for those whose lives touch us directly, even those we fear or dislike the most. Such prayers may not, at first, be much more than the childish utterances of a spoiled five-year-old; but they are a beginning.

Two things happen when we pray for others, whether our prayers are all they ought to be or not. Those we pray for are touched by God, not according to our imperfect prayers but according to his best for them. "For example, we do not know how to pray worthily as sons of God, but his Spirit within us is actually praying for us in those agonizing longings which never find words" (Rom. 8:26). Our prayers are being translated into acceptable terms. Not only that, but we are being helped as we pray. When we turn our attention to God he can communicate with us, can do what needs to be done in our own lives. All we have to do is give him a chance.

As a former locked-in, uncertain, oversensitive person, I can say with conviction that Christ has taken every small prayer of mine for someone else, however childish and imperfect it was, and used it for greater good than I could have imagined. In praying for others I haven't always seen the results I expected, though I have certainly seen great changes for good. But above all he has touched my life when I have prayed. Old bitter memories and wounds have been erased. I've been able to break out of the shell and go out to others in the expectation of being welcomed.

Learning to live without fear of hurt is a process, of course. Part of the process is in accepting the fact that some wounds are inevitable. Accepting these occasional disappointments and affronts without excessive self-pity is far easier once I realize that Christ is healing not only the blows I sustain, but those I give others.

To be afraid of neither life nor death is not possible without Christ. With him, we can say with Paul, "I have become absolutely convinced that neither death nor life . . . has any power to separate us from the love of God in Christ Jesus our Lord!" (Rom. 8:38–39).

—4—

Nobody
Loves a Loser

I would like to be able to say that having found help and strength in time of death that all other problems paled into insignificance. One would think that having found such help that the ordinary rubs, irritations, and common anxieties of life would mean nothing. I discovered to my own dismay that it's not that simple.

After being borne up by what I knew was the grace of God for an otherwise unbearable sorrow, I found I was just as vulnerable to petty worries and annoyances as I had been before. Worse, there was the same old tendency toward self-justification, the same dislike of being wrong, and the same temptation to status seeking. I began to appreciate the truth of Jesus' warning that one day's evil was enough for that day. In the same way, one day's victories are for that day only. There is no carry-over of spiritual success (if one can use that term). We may have gained in strength, wisdom, patience, or faith, but there is never a time when we can draw upon yesterday's resources.

Fear is still very much with us, a daily adversary to be combated. It takes many forms, but one which few of us escape is the fear of failure. I call it that for want of a better term. When I started thinking about it I realized that this particular bogey is not simply the fear of failing in a particular venture or attempt. It's far more profound than that: it is the fear of *being* a failure. Perhaps a better way to say it would be that it is the fear of being thought negligible—a loser. "He's a loser." How many times have you heard that said with varying degrees of contempt? How many times have you or I said it? In our culture it's nearly the worst thing that can be said of anyone, a greater insult than calling a man a cheat or a swindler.

Not too many Christians would admit it, but we are far too afraid of failure to live in a style that fits our profession of faith. We like to succeed, and no wonder—we live in a success-oriented culture. "The American Dream," a phrase often on the lips of politicians and speakers at graduation ceremonies, conveys the picture of a poor boy rising to great heights. The picture used to include the concept of success by virtue of hard work and honesty coupled with moral purity. It was, we are told, based on the Puritan work ethic; but that particular philosophy has been having a thin time of it lately. The American Dream is no longer a picture of success based on certain highly valued character traits—just success, however we come by it.

Our Cultural Presuppositions

That is the cultural climate in which we live. Success is good, being at the top is the best thing in life. Those who don't make it, who have tried and failed or whose feeble attempts at success never really got off the ground are often referred to as losers. This cultural climate presses in on us from all sides, not only overtly but in countless unspoken messages, attitudes, and assumptions we meet every day. That is why it so insidiously creeps into our thinking as Christians.

It can be found masquerading as a very spiritual part of the faith.

We *do* bring into our faith the presuppositions we've grown up with; it would be impossible not to. The old idea that success is the reward of industry and diligence as well as honesty and moral purity has somehow been transmuted into the idea that success itself is the seal of value upon a life. That concept, totally foreign to the Bible, gets into the church because we've brought it with us. It's hard to get rid of.

Making the situation even more problematical is the fact that, for many of us, our first approach to Christianity was in search of help for problems beyond our own strength. We heard the words, "Christ is the answer," and responded to them out of our own helplessness. We assumed that by turning our lives over to Christ we were also handing him everything we had failed to manage, as if he were a divine efficiency expert.

There are those who never get beyond this assumption. They refer every troublesome problem to Jesus' attention and then, having left it to him, go calmly about their business. There will be no more failures in life, because the matter has been turned over to Jesus. And quite often, whatever seemed to be amiss does turn out all right. The point is proven—Jesus is the answer.

But not all our troubles are that simple, not all our sins so easily overcome, not all our situations so easily disposed of. There *are* failures. Some of us struggle for years, for a lifetime, with habits, character weaknesses, or sins that get the best of us time after time. We pray, we agonize, we try again and we are troubled as much by the shame of failing as we are by the problem itself. Failing is so *unspiritual.*

We have fallen into two assumptions because of our

American way of looking at life, neither of them biblical. The first, the one we've already mentioned, is that success is the reward of the deserving. We have forgotten that originally the "deserving" were the hard workers, the honest, dogged, persistent fellows who just kept at it. In transferring this doctrine to the Christian faith, the "deserving" have become those whose spirituality merits God's rewards. The second assumption is also purely American—the belief that if it works, it's good. We are pragmatists at heart. And we've done very well with that philosophy, as a nation. We've built a great country, settled a wilderness, developed immense mechanical and technical expertise, and solved a lot of problems. It's been fatally easy to transfer our faith in the American genius for getting the job done into the spiritual realm. It becomes, in its new Christian context, the belief that when things work out right that's a sign of God's approval.

Our Measuring Sticks

There are two ways of judging whether or not any course of action is right. It can meet all the scriptural standards— and that's not as simple as it sounds. After all, nowhere in the Bible is there a handy list of rules for every situation in life. One must be so at home with the Scripture, so familiar with it that the criteria are part of one's thinking, even part of one's instinctive reactions. There is the whole body of Jesus' teaching. There are the Ten Commandments and the whole of the Old Testament law—which Jesus said were fulfilled in his teaching. There are the letters of the New Testament, full of advice and admonitions about working out the timeless truths of the gospel in everyday life. There is nothing automatic or easy about bringing a course of action to the scrutiny of the Bible.

How very tempting, in view of all this, simply to fall back upon all the generally accepted ideas of whether or not a project is right. And so we usually judge a course of action the second way, the same old way we've always judged— Does it work? And by "work," we mean, Are there immediate and discernible rewards? Is it popular? Is it acceptable to a lot of people? Does it make money? We test our Christian endeavors exactly the same way the maker of a new cereal tests his advertising campaign.

Given this blending of faith in Christ as the "answer" (and we seldom define what we mean by that) and of faith in whatever seems to work best to produce the biggest attendance, or bring in the largest offering, or arouse the greatest emotion, we have produced a Christian climate in which fear of failure is as stultifying as it is outside the church. The concomitant assumption is that financial success on the part of an individual is also a sure indication of his spiritual merit.

Thus the church has gradually developed two parallel and intertwined attitudes: that secular success is a sign of great spirituality, and that we can solve any problem by programing and/or organizing. To say that neither of these assumptions is true lays one open to the charge of being in favor of sloppiness, or spiritual anarchy. It is true that the person who is successful often owes his achievements to hard work and discipline and that some organization, structure, and attention to detail are very necessary to any endeavor. But hard work, discipline, and the most careful planning and organization are neither spiritual nor unspiritual in themselves. They can be good or bad depending upon the goal to which their use is intended. One can be as diligent in pursuing selfish ends as in serving the Lord.

I am not trying to make a case for getting rid of all church organizations, for abandoning plans and programs in favor of just letting things happen. But I am pointing out that we have incorporated into our thinking, both individually and as groups, an unscriptural assumption that we can judge the rightness and effectiveness of our lives and works by secular standards. We cannot. We have been given quite another way of evaluating what we do and how we live.

The Biblical View

When we examine the Bible carefully to see what God's standards for us are, we find that—unlike ourselves—the Bible is not particularly concerned with success as we think of success. It is not even concerned with whether or not what we do "works." Paul pointed out that the gospel was unacceptable to the Jews, who were looking for miraculous proofs, and to the Greeks who wanted an intellectual panacea. Those who had committed themselves to Christ, he said, were nobodies in the eyes of the world. He went on to remark that God had chosen what the world calls foolish and weak to shame the wise and strong. The "foolish" and the "weak" were the Christians he was writing to and I suspect that they didn't like being called those terms any more than we do. But the point of Paul's argument, found in the first three chapters of his first letter to the church at Corinth, was that our faith is not merely human, but rests upon *super* human resources—the wisdom and strength of God himself.

In submitting ourselves to the guidance of the Bible we are not going contrary to ordinary rules of prudence or wisdom, we are going beyond them. We are enlisted in the service of a Lord who is either ignored or despised by most of the world. In so doing we have already embarked upon a life which would appear to those outside it to be weak and foolish—we are already failures.

Besides that, we have pledged ourselves to the kind of life which pleases God, not man, and pleasing God will certainly mean that many of the methods used in order to achieve success by those around us will not be for us. But when we go through the process I've described—bringing into our faith the ordinary secular ideas of success and workability—we are bringing in an element which is totally contrary to the very basis of our faith. Jesus was not a success by the world's standards.

In order to combat the insidious temptation to evaluate our own lives and our Christian community by secular notions of success, we have to continually remind ourselves of the fact that Christianity itself is in opposition to the world.

I believe that the first question we must ask about any attitude, plan, project, or proposal is, "Does this square with what I know of God's will as I read it in the Scripture?" We must ask that even before we pray. It is obvious that however hard we pray, God is never going to lead us in any way that is contrary to what he has already clearly revealed. If it can't meet that first test, there's no use even praying. The question is answered negatively and the proposal is out.

Once we feel assured of going ahead, however, there is a further test. Every part of the implementation of whatever we do must meet the same requirements. We do *not* believe that the end justifies the means, but that the means must be consistent with the end.

Freedom from Fear of Failure

When we use these tests in our individual lives we discover that we are free to move ahead with assurance. There is marvelous liberty in doing something because it is right. For one thing, we usually find that what is right is also what we like doing. It's amazing how many people embark on a course of action not because they enjoy it or because it is right, but because it is socially acceptable or because it will bring money or prestige or both. Those are the wrong reasons for doing anything, and they breed an unholy fear of failure. In fact, they not only breed fear of failure but they are the product of that very same fear. To get rid of any of those reasons for doing a thing is to be freed of an incubus.

When one is doing something because he likes doing it

and because it's right he is not only less likely to dissipate his energies worrying about whether or not he will fail, but he is far more likely to do whatever he is doing well. He may never achieve success in the usually accepted idea of the term, which means making a great deal of money or becoming very well known; but he will be a success in the only true sense of the word—doing a job well.

Any Christian who takes his commitment to Christ seriously must come to grips with the question, "Do I want success in the eyes of the world, which may mean using methods not compatible with my Christian faith, or do I want to be absolutely true to God in every area of my life even if it means sacrificing advancement or money?" We must be mature enough in our faith, and in our thinking, to accept the fact that God's standards of honesty and integrity are not those of the secular world in which we live; and that we must make a choice.

Jesus was very blunt about presenting the alternatives to his listeners. He called them to an allegiance to God but always with a warning that it would mean giving up their allegiance to any other gods they had. There was a price to pay for following him.

The price, which is still required of his followers, is that in accepting God's standards of success we may be, and often are, obliged to forego the rewards which come to those who let no scruples stand in their way. To be acceptable to God can mean being a failure in the eyes of the world.

The Church—Another Pressure Group?

It is at this point that we find we are dealing not only with the fears and hopes of individuals, but with the way we are as a Christian community. Although we come to Christ alone and make our decision to be his or to go it on our own, we do not live the Christian life alone. We come into a community of believers. Each one's personal relationship with

Christ, important as it is, is incomplete without his relationships within the Christian community. We need each other.

We need each other's help, strength, and affirmation because we probably will not get it outside the church. One of my friends resigned from a coveted position because he could not go along with the shabby morality and unethical practices of his firm; nearly everyone who knew of it thought he was an idiot. "Why did he have to give up a good thing for some dumb academic issue?" asked one man. "You can be as honest as possible, but his ideas are out of the ark!" The words may have been different but the sentiments of most of his colleagues were the same—a man is a fool to allow scruples to stand in the way of advancement.

That is not to be wondered at, it's the way the world is. We all know it. Only in the Christian community, the family of God's people, can things be different. There we can find acceptance based not on what we have achieved in the way of position, power, or money but on what we are.

But can we? An honest look at ourselves as Christians, at our churches and various groupings and subdivisions, brings us to the realization that all too often the church of Christ has adopted the same ideas of success that are part of the secular world. There is often no help in the church for the man or woman looking for acceptance. Often there is little help in dealing with the problems a Christian faces in earning a living because he will be judged no differently than he would be outside the church.

I believe we must come to terms with the fact that the biblical portrait of a life which endeavors to meet God's demands for goodness is not that of our contemporary world. We must grapple with the hard questions of morality and ethics in the business and professional world as individuals; but we must also face these issues and cope with them *as a church*—as the people of God in the world.

As it is now, with the secular attitude toward success and

failure often being taken into our churches and invested
with a sort of spiritual varnish, we face the stresses of life
in a highly competitive society without much help from the
Christian community. In fact, we all too frequently meet
with exactly the same pressure, the same reverence for success and consequent contempt for those who don't meet the
standard, that we have to face every working day.

Getting Rid of the Success Syndrome

There is no quick and easy cure for this, of course. Recog-
nizing a problem is not the same as dealing with it, though
we are tempted to believe so. We need more than small
group sessions titled, "What is a failure?" or seminars on the
Christian's faith in a secular world. You don't get rid of a bad
attitude by making it the subject of a discussion group,
though that is very helpful. The only effective way of coping
with any problem is by doing whatever is right and necessary
according to our understanding of biblical standards *as each
situation arises.*

The first step, of course, is to acknowledge the fact that
we are prone to fall into unchristian attitudes about success
and failure. But after that, talking and discussion are really
no help unless they take place in specific situations, about
specific issues. Fortunately, many of these issues are being
dealt with in a far more realistic and far more Christian manner than most of us have managed, by younger Christians.
They already have a healthy disregard for much of the "establishment" thinking so they have an advantage to begin
with.

One young friend is working as an apprentice cabinet
builder because he likes working with wood and has decided
that he'd rather do what he enjoys than try for a more pres-
tigious, but less compatible, kind of work. Another man who
came here from Europe as a stone mason gave up his plans

to be a history teacher because he realized that he really preferred working with stone and had planned to teach because it seemed more acceptable socially.

We will not all have such clear-cut choices to make, but we'll have choices. It may be nothing more weighty than whether I will prepare a company dinner of beef Wellington because it is impressive and my reputation as a hostess will be enhanced, or a dinner of goulash because it's delicious and will fit my budget better. This may seem ridiculous in the light of all we have said about success and failure, but everything we do, every choice we make, is in some sense conditioned by what we think will make us successful—or stamp us as failures. When we accept the fact that "making it" as far as the rest of the world goes is not necessarily making it with God then we are on the right track.

We may be finally free of the dreadful horror of being thought a loser when we remind ourselves that, apart from Christ, we are all losers in God's eyes. All the promises of victory, all the assurances that we will never be downed, all the stirring commands to buck up and live according to our faith were given to us not as people inherently able to make it alone, but as people who are triumphant because we are *in Christ*. He is the one who is victorious. It isn't true, after all, that nobody loves a loser—God does. His is the only kind of love that can take a loser and make him a winner.

—5—

The World
Within the Church

There are two ways in which we usually respond to things that frighten us: we either meet the fear head-on, or we retreat. We've already seen how many threats to life and happiness all of us face. The picture of the world painted by the writers of the New Testament may be summed up in the words of John who wrote in his first letter, "For the whole world system, based as it is on men's primitive desires, their greedy ambitions and the glamours of all that they think splendid, is not derived from the Father at all, but from the world itself" (1 John 2:16).

From the beginning of the church's life Christians have known the world to be opposed to the rule of God. Most of the dangers we most fear are part of that world and it makes living by the gospel a precarious business. And so we are afraid.

We're desperately afraid of being closely involved in *the world*. We speak of it in italicized tones. We long to be perfectly safe, to be immune from the dangers the rest of the world must cope with. If we have to accept a certain amount of suffering from disease and accident, at least (we tell ourselves) we don't have to rub shoulders with the unsanctified, the unwashed, or the unrespectable.

The Ambivalent Church

The church has always been ambivalent in the matter of its calling. Is the church to be a body of believers coming together for mutual help and corporate worship and then dispersing to function as God's representatives wherever they are in the world, or to be a clubby fellowship of people who are all exactly alike? The church is ambivalent about its calling no doubt because human beings are ambivalent in just the same way. *Our desire to be safe is often opposed and inhibiting to our urge to achieve and even to adventure.*

Perhaps this goes back to the garden of Eden, that perfect place where nothing was lacking, not even the fellowship with God unclouded by estrangement. When the tempter invited Adam and Eve to taste the forbidden fruit and said it would endow them with the knowledge of good and evil, what could have gone through their minds? They had no reason to believe they would ever be in want or lack of anything—life had been complete. But at the first hint that there was something they didn't have anxiety sprang into being. In the face of all the evidence to the contrary they apparently were convinced their lives would lack something without this fruit. The issue was very clear: to believe God, who had told them not to touch the fruit lest they die, and who had supplied them with everything to sustain life and even to beautify it; or to believe the devil who told them they would be like God; that he had withheld the fruit because they would then be like him.

"Gracious," she might have said, "we'd certainly better have this knowledge of good and evil. Who knows when something might come up which we can't handle the way we are? It's all very well for the Lord God to put us in charge but what will we do if he goes off and leaves it all to us?"

The outcome, of course, was a far more dangerous life than they had known in the garden. The anxiety that prompted them to eat the fruit now had real, not imaginary, ills to focus on. They were thrust out into the world where we have been ever since.

The church was called to reverse what happened in the garden. Existing in the world, without the ideal situation of the garden, we are called to exhibit the trust in God that Adam and Eve failed to show. What would have been easy for them is difficult for us. But that is what we are called to do.

The Ambivalent World

"The world" isn't everything that exists outside the church, it's everything that exists outside God's rule; and it is ambivalent. The world which we so fear, and emulate, is the world of which we are told to beware: "Never give your hearts to this world or to any of the things in it. A man cannot love the Father and love the world at the same time. For the whole world system, based as it is on men's primitive desires, their greedy ambitions and the glamour of all that they think splendid, is not derived from the Father at all, but from the world itself" (1 John 2:15–16). It is also the world God loved so much that he gave his only begotten Son to save. It is "this dark world," according to Paul, and the world into which Jesus sent his disciples. It is also the world God created and once called "good."

Portrayed as it is in the Bible *the world is man's system of values rather than God's.* It is what we have left when we leave God out of our lives. It is also *the world God loved* so much he gave his only Son for its salvation. It is the world for which Christ died. And it is made up of men and women who, however indifferent to God they may be, however given to selfishness and the gratification of their own lusts, are candidates for redemption. God loves them. The Bible does not say he loves us once we have admitted our need for him, but that he loves those who are still far from loving him. That's "the world"—opposed to God, yet loved by him and capable of being redeemed. Seen in this light it is easy to perceive how we must live in the world and never despise it—after all, it's a good thing gone wrong; how we must use all our ingenuity and compassion to reach it for Christ, but never adopt its standards. We are, in short, to be in it but not of it.

We Must Be in the World—Not of It

There may or may not be a spiritual principle here. The fact remains that whenever we refuse to be *in it*, to work in it, make our gospel relevant in it, and be faithful to Christ in it, whenever we retreat into some safe and select gathering of like-minded people, a dreadful transformation takes place: *we become of it.* It may be that the only way we can keep ourselves open to the help God has for us is to be in an exposed place—so exposed that the dangers are obvious, and our need for his help unmistakable.

The moment we begin to imagine ourselves safe, safe in our self-created little societies, our own tiny world, we fall victim to the very attitudes and tensions and delusions we have tried to escape.

And that is why the religious groups which have been most determinedly separate from the world have tended to develop quite worldly attitudes. The fact that those attitudes are masked behind a surface piety makes them all the more deadly. They are evidence of a disease whose symptoms we never recognize because we're looking for quite a different manifestation.

C. S. Lewis remarked in his *Screwtape Letters* that of the three standard temptations—the world, the flesh and the devil—the world is by far the most dangerous because it's the most subtle. It may also be the most dangerous because we fear it for the wrong reasons.

But we are afraid of the world, in a totally mistaken way. We are afraid we'll be hurt by it, laughed at, or despised for our faith. We draw our boundaries in an effort to be safe from the world but we are afraid of the wrong kind of harm. Jesus warned us not to fear those who can kill the body (and that is certainly the most extreme danger we fear) but him who has power to cast into hell. We are afraid of sustaining hurts in our bodies or our feelings—or our pocketbooks—when we really ought to be afraid of being drawn away from Christ. *There* is the real danger. And in our obsessive fear of all the wrong things, we fall into that very snare.

Something happens when a group turns in upon itself, the same sort of thing that takes place when an individual turns inward. The church which ignores the clear command of Scripture to send its members out into the needy world around it becomes, like any self-centered person, obsessed with its own workings.

A friend used to tell me about one of her relatives who displayed just such an obsession. She was absorbed by her digestive processes, and friends and acquaintances were invariably met with a detailed account of what had been happening to her stomach and bowels. Because she was so absorbed by her own insides, she of course took no interest in anything outside herself and was totally insensitive to the boredom she induced wherever she went. People laughed at her, of course, and avoided her whenever they could.

There is a correlation here between such a self-obsessed person (whether it is digestion or psyche) and a defensive, walled-in church. Lacking that natural sphere of activity which is the world around it, the church expends all its energy upon itself. As that dreary woman talked incessantly about her digestion, such a church talks of nothing but its own affairs. It has become a ghetto.

When we try to build a safe little society apart from the world in order to be safe we succeed only in creating a small microcosm of the world around us. We never escape its dangers—we simply duplicate them.

In our culture today, tremendous tension is produced by the need to succeed in order to be accepted. We have already discussed what that does to us. It's not possible to totally escape that pressure; we have to live and work in the world.

How tempting it is, then, to make the church one place where we can be free of all we find so disagreeable in our everyday lives. We will have our own group of people whose faith and goals are the same. The church becomes a haven for us, not just for a few hours on Sunday and occasionally during the week, but it becomes a permanent refuge.

Inevitably, we create within such a group the same pressure to succeed, though the standards may be different. Success or failure may be measured by far different standards than one would find in the business world, but the fact that they exist at all means the world is alive and well within the church.

The moment any standards of acceptance other than that of commitment to Christ and adherence to his gospel become current in a group an attitude of tension and anxiety is produced. It's the same attitude that is prevalent outside the church. After all, we are under constant pressure to succeed in business, to be popular, to be successful and that makes us fearful. The church ought to be the one place we are free from those pressures, where we are accepted simply as ourselves without decoration. But if it imposes the very same pressure to "be" somebody special, to be recognized as worthwhile because of one's success or other attainments, then there is no release from the constant pressure to compete, to be "better than."

There is in most of us a hankering to be thought well of—to be looked up to. Innocent enough if all we want is just to be accepted for ourselves, it becomes deadly when we want to be accepted as *better than* the others. It's not new. Many of Paul's letters—Galatians, Colossians, and the letters to Corinth especially—were written partly to combat the insidious workings of men who set themselves up as his rivals. He objected to their false doctrines and saw quite clearly that their objectives were personal, to be preeminent.

As he finished writing his letter to the Galatians, he comments wryly: "If a man thinks he is 'somebody,' he is deceiving himself, for that very thought proves that he is nobody" (Gal. 6:3). The apostle John had the same trouble—we see a glimpse of his youthful fire in this sentence written to Gaius, who might have been the leader of a small church in Asia Minor: "I did write a letter to the church, but Diotrephes, who wants to be head of everything, does not recognize us! If I do come to you, I shall not forget his actions nor the slanderous things he has said against us. And it doesn't stop there, alas, for although he wants to be leader he refuses the duty of welcoming the brothers himself, and stops those who would like to do so—he even excommunicates them!" (3 John 9–10).

Diotrephes' behavior seems a little extreme. We would hardly excommunicate those who pose a threat to our supremacy. Since God does not recognize gradations of sin, however, it may be that he regards our maneuvering for position, our sycophantic adulation of influential personages, and our eagerness to get moneyed people into our churches as no less deadly than murder or adultery. In fact, he might regard snobbery as a kind of adultery; giving our allegiance to the world instead of to him.

If this is so, how are we going to handle the fear which makes us snuggle up to people because they are socially prominent or successful in business or a profession? And how do we cope with these false standards when we find them in the church?

No doubt the first impulse of many of us, products as we are of an age which handles every problem by forming a committee to study it, would be to form a group of activists or dissidents; like-minded people who would give talks on the evils of snobbery and exhort those around them to get out into the world and do something for Christ. That may be the way of our contemporary culture, but it is not the style of the New Testament.

Jesus, though he spoke to thousands, called upon every man and woman to do what is right as an individual. Paul, though he wrote to churches, and certainly spoke to us all as members of a body united as much as a physical body, demanded right attitudes and behavior of individuals. The group is healthy as each member is healthy. We do not live outside the body of Christ, or apart from it, but we must each function properly or the entire body will suffer.

It seems to me, then, that my responsibility to God—and to the church—is to face my own attitudes and examine them in the light of what I know of Scripture. For instance, when I am asked to do something in the church I must ask myself, "Is this what God wants me to do? If I accept, will it be to serve him, or because I want to impress certain people?" In a discussion, do I speak what I believe to be the truth even though I know it may offend influential personages? Do I tailor my life-style to please God, or to impress others? Am I recommending that Mr. ———— be on the church board because I believe he will do a faithful and conscientious job, or because I think it would give us a certain prestige to be able to say, "Yes, Mr. ——— is a member of our board"?

To look at my own motives with any degree of honesty means not only reading the Bible carefully, asking what it says *to me*, to this situation, but praying very frankly for help.

Perhaps one reason we find it so difficult to refrain from hiding out in the church instead of being useful to God in the world, so difficult to speak honestly and value each other fairly without snobbery, is that we don't admit these sins even to God.

We must face the fact that there isn't any instant method of making the church—any church—what it ought to be. Whatever we see to be wrong, whatever needs to be changed, the change begins with each one of us. This does not mean that nothing will take place in the larger scene, that we are restricted to small efforts which will never get very far. We tend to assume that what one person does will be negligible because we live in a culture that worships bigness and large numbers.

The New Testament does not share that assumption. It always speaks to us as individuals and makes demands upon us. We are not to wait for a parade to form before following Christ. We are called upon, instead, to fall in behind him whether there is a parade or not. And there is no guarantee that there will be.

However, I've observed that when one Christian begins to feel strongly, and then to act upon what he is convinced is right, nearly always he soon discovers he is not alone— there are others who are going the same way. Perhaps some of them are too timid to speak up—to begin the parade. But once someone leads the way, they take heart and join in.

We will never succeed in completely eradicating all

evidences of worldliness in the church. That would require a degree of perfection in us which will be ours only in eternity. But we can keep at it.

In addition to continually examining our own attitudes in the light of what we know of the truth, we must avoid doing things in the church simply because they are nice activities which we'd rather share with our own group than with those outside. The business of the church is to put its members out into the world equipped to live as mature, responsible men and women of the faith. It is *not* to provide a life complete with all the diversions of contemporary life one might enjoy in the secular world.

There really isn't enough time to do all we have to do in order to carry out our mission of bringing Christ to the world as well as taking care of all the social needs of our members. If we try to do the latter, we will almost certainly neglect the former. We must choose which we are going to do—whether we will be faithful to Christ's command to be *in the world but not of it* and all that implies in the way of training and preparation—or devote our time to making the church a safe and comfortable substitute for the world outside.

—6—

The Church in Hiding

A man who has spent twenty-five years training salesmen tells me that he can teach anyone to sell with one exception —the person who is afraid. Fear immobilizes like no other emotion can. The picture I drew in the last chapter is that of a church immobilized by such fear. It has turned in upon itself. It has isolated itself from the world and calls it "spirituality" or "being separated from the unclean thing," but it is really fear. This is not a portrait of any specific church, but a composite picture of many Christians in many churches.

The pity of it is that so many churches of the evangelical branch of the church universal have chosen to take this route. Of course, when we have done so, it hasn't been a deliberate and knowing choice. We have simply avoided facing the rigors of our Christian calling by means of fuzzy, and wishful, thinking. We have convinced ourselves that being his witnesses in the world means seeing to it that the gospel is preached in our pulpits, putting on evangelistic campaigns and sending deputation teams to jails and skid row missions. The more daring of us hand out tracts or seize every opportunity to "give our testimony for Christ."

Witnessing More Than a Technique

These endeavors, taken by themselves, are all good and converts are won by such means. But they are not the *primary* means of reaching the world for Christ; and when they become a substitute for real involvement, they are very bad for us. They may or may not be bad for those on the receiving end, depending on the degree of sensitivity with which we employ them. But they are certainly bad for us because we so easily deceive ourselves into thinking this is all God requires of us. By such self-deception we also become blind to the worldliness we have brought into the church.

We think of the gospel as being only the message of salvation, or whatever presentation of it is made to those outside the faith. But when we confine all our real living—our social intercourse, our friendships, and all our leisure time—to what goes on within the Christian community, what kind of relationship can we have with those outside? It's a very shallow one. We don't get close enough to anyone outside "our group" to become involved in his problems.

I believe that one of the reasons so many of us are anemic in our faith, petty, secular, and timid in reaching those outside, is that our isolation from our world has, of necessity, forced us to create a pseudo world of our own. But our faith was not designed for a protected, closed existence.

Real Life Is Risky

Christianity is for life—life lived in the real world, which is dangerous and hostile to God and at the same time hopelessly lost. It is meant for the knocks and tumbles of everyday encounters in that world. That's why we are sometimes confused by its mingling of reassurances and warnings; we like the reassurances, but wish the warnings weren't necessary. Perhaps (we hope) they're meant for those in extraordinary situations: missionaries, crusaders, martyrs called to live in desperate times quite unlike ours.

We often think this way because we really do not want to face the fact that life has always been dangerous—for the Christian and the non-Christian alike. There is no way to eliminate all the risks from living. Of course, the major danger was done away with when Christ took upon himself the burden of our sins and paid for them on the cross. The resurrection stands as God's crowning affirmative word to us, assuring us that we are destined for eternity, not for extinction.

Again and again Jesus advised his disciples to "fear not" because their lives were in God's hands. They would survive all the risks, troubles, and disasters which seemed so threatening. They were very much like us, however. Ultimate safety is all very well, but wouldn't it be better to have things straightened out *now* too? "Lord, will you at this time bring in the kingdom?" was their naïve question, showing how deeply they longed for everything to be put right immediately, so life (and presumably the conversion of the world) could go on without undue hazard.

Jesus' reply was, in effect, "That's none of your business. You just get on with the job you've been given, which is to be my witnesses in the world." Or, as Earl Palmer put it, "I'm in management, you're in sales." What we have done when we attempt to make the church into a special, small, and safe little world, is to try to get into management, with a consequent neglect of sales. As every good salesman knows, the way to sell products is to get out where the customers are. Now that's perhaps a poor analogy for witnessing, because we are not really selling anything. We are, instead, demonstrating something.

We all know that the image evoked by the word *salesmanship* is of a brash, insensitive, frequently unscrupulous person bent on forcing his product down the throats of hesitant or unwilling customers by any possible means. We think of blaring television commercials, obviously exaggerated claims, and the word *hucksterism*. That's not for the gospel—it's cheap and shallow.

But it is true that there is some worldly knowledge we might do well to pay attention to and it is this: the good salesman knows that the one thing which will do him in is fear. He may make any number of blunders and still do a good job of selling, but if he is afraid he's done for. We need to learn that. Fear makes us totally ineffective.

Who's in Charge Here?

If we *are* living, as many of us are, in small, guarded enclaves, fenced away from the world around us, we need to hear again the words Jesus said to his disciples when they wanted to know about the kingdom. What they were really saying was, "Aren't you going to make life safe for us now?" And he said to them—and to us—"Stop worrying about how the Father is managing the world and do your job in it." He had assured them he would be with them as they went about his business, and that power had been given him. The power was to enable them to preach his message—to be witnesses —not to guarantee a trouble-free life.

What happens when we forget that fact and live in our little ghettos, is not only that we become worldly—*of* the world, rather than *in* it—but we subtly debase the gospel, converting it from the word of God to us in the world into a rule book for membership in a religious country club.

The church has always had to fight this tendency, and has done so with varying degrees of success. Our task is to make the eternal gospel evident in our lives and words, and we have to do it in the culture of our own day. That's quite a job in itself, and it is complicated by the fact that as products of a particular culture we will find it difficult not to read some of our cultural presuppositions into the faith. We do it quite innocently; it isn't a conscious process at all. And part of maturing as a Christian is the business of learning the difference between our own ideas with their cultural assumptions and biblical truths. That is why reading and studying the Bible goes on all our lives. We never get to the point where we can say, "There, I have it! I've learned all there is to know and don't need to read *that* any more." We are frequently shocked by passages we've read many times, as we suddenly see them without the cultural wrappings with which we've had them safely covered.

The Dream of Safety Pops Up Again

One of the cultural wrappings is the belief that life ought to be—and can be—safe from all possible harm. We bring our contemporary thinking about the ideal life as one of absolute safety and absolute comfort right into our Christianity. We then interpret what the Bible has to say to us in the light of those ideas. We slide quite easily from the fact that Christ died to save us from our sins, to save us from our lostness, into the notion that he died to save us from discomfort as well.

Then we set about making our lives as comfortable and safe as possible. We have our groups of like-minded believers, and we stay within them except for brief forays into the world. We have to earn a living, do our shopping, and carry on necessary business out there in that alien world, but as much as possible we confine our real lives to our own special group, which has become a subculture.

Fear Makes Us Provincial . . .

We somehow feel that culture must be made safe and kept safe so outsiders can't get in—unless they adopt our tenets and fit in with us comfortably. The cultures within the church vary, of course, and the differences are a source of division and dissention within the body of Christ. It isn't theological differences which divide Christians as much as a deep suspicion of each other's different life-styles. We are afraid of those whose way of worshiping and whose life-style are different from ours. That attitude is a direct carry-over from secular thinking and is contrary to both the letter and the spirit of the New Testament. I suppose the earliest recorded instance of such provincialism is in the Gospel of John. The woman Jesus met at a well in Samaria began a religious discussion by saying, "Now our ancestors worshiped on this hillside, but you Jews say that Jerusalem is the place where men ought to worship—" (John 4:20).

Jesus interrupted her with a stern reminder that men ought to worship God neither "on this hillside" nor "in Jerusalem," but in spirit and in truth. There is no evidence anywhere in the New Testament that God prefers a liturgical to a nonliturgical service, or likes gospel hymns better than Bach chorales. Both are cultural expressions of the same faith.

We are bound to express our worship of him in our own culture, whatever it is, and we will of course be more comfortable in some groups than in others. What is really vital is that we worship God as truly and as honestly as we know how; that we offer him our very best. For some people their very best is a free, fairly informal service without much structure. For others, the beauty and timelessness of a liturgical service meet both the need to worship and to be fed.

Either way, God is worshiped and his people are in fellowship together. The one thing that can corrupt both the worship and the fellowship more quickly than anything else is for the people to assume that *their* kind of service, *their* way of worshiping God, is the only or the best way.

. . . and Snobbish

Once we adopt that attitude we begin to make our Christian culture safe, because we invest it with all the reverence and loyalty we ought to give to Christ alone. We end up, quite frequently, by putting our faith and trust not in Christ at all, but in our segregated little worlds, the small societies, in which we live and move and have our being.

This deadly exclusiveness was the subject of a satirical revue written and produced some years ago by a small group of people at the Hollywood Presbyterian Church. My son, Dr. Darrell Guder, wrote the libretto and the words to some of the songs, one of which was called "The Group." It went like this:

> What a dreadful thing it is
> That there are people in our midst
> Who are saying God is dead,
> When it is obvious
> That He's very much alive
> And a member of Our Group,
> And you can find him too
> If you'll be one of us.
>
> *Chorus*
> If Jesus were on earth today
> We know He'd gravitate our way,
> For we're the kind of people he would choose.
> We know He'd feel at home with us.
> It's clear He'd never roam from us,
> With us around His cause just could not lose!
> We're the nearest thing to heav'n on earth He'd find—
> We're the very sort of kin and kith
> Christ should be seen in public with,
> We're the salt, the light, the faithful—we're His kind.

The song went on with some very pungent verses and we sang it to a catchy tune written by Paul Killian. The really interesting reactions we got to the show were a prime il-lustration of our passion for conformity. There were, of course, those who liked the show and got the point—I sup-pose a majority of those who saw it. Others reacted with violent anger, not because they disagreed with the point of view of the show, but because they thought that making fun of the foibles and silliness of Christians was just the same as making fun of God.

. . . and Humorless

One woman said reproachfully, "I just don't think you should hold up Christians to ridicule. We are trying to do the best we can and we need all the help we can get."

"Yes," I said, "I agree we need help. But don't you think that it's good for us to see through our little pretenses, and to be able to laugh at ourselves? Maybe if we recognize some of our peccadillos we'll be able to get rid of them."

"I just don't think it's right to point out our faults," she said stubbornly, "after all, we're better than 'the world.' Why didn't you do a nice show telling about some of the good things about the church?"

One of the results of taking one's own culture too seri-ously, and assuming that the way we do things is the way God wishes everyone would do things, is that we become humorless. There is nothing so fatal to a sense of balance as a total lack of humor, and we are usually saved from ex-cesses by being able to laugh at ourselves. When we can't—when we become defensive and touchy—that's a danger signal and ought to alert us to the fact that we're treating as sacred something which is merely cultural.

As a matter of fact, the urge to be completely safe is about the most sobering motive there is; no wonder when we try to make our little Christian world safe we lose all our humor and lightness. We become very dull people, which is a major defeat for any real witness we might have.

. . . *and Worldly*

I suppose the next step is inevitable—our particular culture has got to be kept safe, guarded, and protected from any invasion from outside.

The result is a worldly group of Christians living a segregated life—so insulated and buttressed against any touch with life on the outside that they lead very artificial lives. They become preoccupied with small, worrisome problems which have nothing to do with the world in which we live, and thus remain frighteningly ignorant of the thinking and attitudes of those outside.

The compulsion to create a safe milieu for ourselves, as if Christianity were a tender plant unsuited to the rigors of contemporary life, begets a series of attitudes which one can find in any separated society. The provincialism, snobbishness, and worldliness which result from living a ghetto-like existence appear to be picayune faults compared to other evils. They have none of the awful grandeur of pride which sets itself up against God, or lust for power so strong it crushes lives, or avarice, or vengefulness. However, snobbishness and worldliness are sins, though they may be derivative. In this case they are the product of fear, a fear which perpetuates the human cussedness in all of us.

The purpose of the church is to help us grow up into maturity as Christians as well as to carry the message that Christ has come to the world. But we cannot do either as long as we are inhibited by fear. Fear prevents us from being what we ought to be as a community of believers, and keeps us from venturing out to encounter the challenges of our contemporary society.

—7—

Change

or Manipulate

Fear produces two parallel phobias: resistance to change and manipulation. In trying to decide which comes first, fear of change or the manipulation to prevent change, we face a problem much like that of the chicken or the egg. It's hard to tell which *does* come first. Perhaps the determination to stave off any change comes first and results in manipulation; but our fear of change is often hidden, and the manipulation is obvious.

We see this happen in a church which has become a ghetto and begun to create its own safe world. No matter how much is said and quoted from the Bible about "trusting in God," and "waiting upon the Lord," the trust and the waiting are purely verbal. The urge to make sure that all goes well and that nothing intrudes into the tidy world of separated saints breeds an atmosphere in which manipulation is inevitable.

It is never acknowledged, of course. Those who are busiest arranging matters to their satisfaction quite often say, with sincerity, that the Holy Spirit has told them just what to do. As a matter of fact, the Holy Spirit gets the credit (or blame) for our own thinking and plotting. Where Flip

87

Wilson's Geraldine claims, "the devil made me do it," we are prone to say, "the Holy Spirit told me so."

Do We Really Trust God?

Behind our tendency to arrange affairs to suit ourselves lies a fear that we refuse to acknowledge—the fear that if we don't see to it, God will not preserve our little world just as we like it. The zeal with which so many of us guard the affairs of our ghettos is not so much enthusiasm as it is lack of trust in God. It may be that from time to time we suspect that he is not nearly as interested in preserving the status quo as we are.

What usually results is that the group which runs things in a church becomes very defensive about its prerogatives, very reluctant to bring in new people, and, of course, slow to accept changes. Younger men and women are regarded with suspicion unless they appear willing to go along with things the way they have always been. In one church— which had been successfully run for years by a fairly small group of men without much interference from the membership—the congregation finally became concerned enough to make itself heard. Meetings were no longer placid and dull affairs where everyone simply voted "Yes" at the proper time. People stood up and said what they thought, offered motions, and refused to vote as they had been used to in the past. Two members of the board got together to discuss the catastrophe and what could be done about it. One of them finally slapped his hand on the table and said, "We'll just have to dig our heels in!"

These are not wicked men who are trying to keep the righteous down—they think they *are* the righteous. They are honestly bewildered when their decisions are questioned. After all, haven't they run things for years and years? Why this sudden disturbance? They can't see that it's no longer possible to create a safe little world-within-a-world and run it to suit ourselves. We know too much. The constant barrage of news from all over the world which we read in the papers, see on television, and hear on the radio has made the dream of a safe haven for Christians suddenly very insubstantial. We cannot help being aware of our world, whether we like it nor not.

Keeping the Church Safe

But for those who have created a Christian subculture and whose safety and serenity depend on the preservation of that culture, such knowledge evokes only fear. Rather than concern for a world which obviously needs help and is looking desperately for solutions, these pious people react to every disturbance or social change with a stubborn determination to make sure there is one haven of safety—their church. Their fear of what is going on in the world—its very real dangers and problems—becomes fear of any change at all.

All change, even in such minor matters as the order of church service, the hymns that are sung, or committee procedures, appears to them to be the thin end of the wedge. It must be sternly resisted, and they do so with the zeal of the Lord's anointed.

Discussing this very situation recently, a young man said, "Nonsense, it isn't that they're so afraid of change that the men who run things hang on so tightly, it's just that they like power, they like being important even in a small social group like our church, and they aren't going to let go of their power easily."

That may be true but why are such men so fond of power? Original sin? I don't know any churchmen in positions of influence and power who are deliberately and consciously clinging to power just because they like it. Most of them give hours of time working for ends they honestly believe to be good for the kingdom. They do not fit the stereotype of the proud, cold, self-righteous Pharisee most often found in novels and movies. They are good men.

But they are deluded by the notion that the church ought to be a haven of safety from all we find disagreeable in the world around us. They are trying to preserve a social culture because it's the atmosphere which they find most comfortable and comforting. Everything they experience in their daily lives outside the Christian ghetto confirms their fear and dislike of the changes taking place. Just watching the evening news on television can be a very depressing experience. Old standards are not only ignored, but jeered. Respect for authority seems practically nonexistent. Long accepted standards of morality are considered quaint and old-fashioned, violence is commonplace; no wonder the world is an alarming spectacle; no wonder so many are determined to keep their own Christian world safe from such changes.

We Must Remember Our Goals

It won't work, of course. Change is inevitable because men grow old and die and another generation with different ideas and methods comes along. But the attempt to preserve things as they are in any group—especially within the Christian community—can keep both those who are fighting to prevent change and those who would welcome it involved in a struggle for power which has nothing to do with the real business of the church. That is why we need to guard against either standing pat for the way things are or kicking and fighting to take over and change matters. A struggle for power in any church is always a defeat for the real work we have to do.

Help for this problem—which is distressingly common—does not lie in trying to convince those of the establishment that they ought to be more flexible, or in advising impatient young people to go slow. Instead, we need to remind ourselves that the real business of the church is to do two things: to proclaim the good news of the gospel to the world, and to nurture and strengthen the members of the Christian community.

In every age that double task has had to use methods suitable to the condition of its own world. Those change from time to time but the goals are the same. In our anxiety to create and maintain a safe environment, we tend to lose sight of our goals. When we are primarily concerned with our own affairs, with the organization, structure, and workings of our church (and especially with its preservation the way we think it ought to be) our fear of life's ordinary risks grows. That fear always produces an unhealthy climate of manipulation.

The Attempt to Control Is Fatal

We keep the fear hidden away, even from ourselves; we hate to admit that we *are* afraid, since it is so obviously not one of the Christian virtues. I believe that we are often reluctant to examine our fear because of an even deeper anxiety—that our faith is not what we think it to be. We are not so much afraid the gospel isn't true as we are that its truth, faced squarely, will show up the holes in our own version. And the temptation to adapt the faith to a sanguine expectation of the good life is very strong.

We can't control history or avoid the pitfalls of the business world, but we can, we think, make sure all goes well in our Christian world. And so we manipulate.

I remember being at a women's retreat when one woman, evidently moved by the message, began to weep and told the group that she had worked very hard in a local PTA, but had come to realize that all her hard work was really manipulation. She felt convicted of having influenced people by half-truths, sometimes by withholding facts, not for a bad end, but to achieve what she thought was a good result. It was still manipulation.

"Oh, well," a friend said as we were talking about a situation in which the same thing went on in church, "you've just got to expect that. After all, we're human—people like to run things, we all tend to color the truth a little to make things go our way. We've just got to be realistic about the church—it's run about the same way any other organization is."

She was right in saying that's the way churches often are run, but I think she was wrong in saying that's the way it has to be. It doesn't have to be and it's not true of all churches.

Facing Our Own Responsibility

It seems to me that we evangelicals often slide from a theological fact—that we are sinful people who never achieve perfection in this life—to an easy assumption that therefore our failures and shortcomings are all right. We excuse shabby behavior which ought to horrify us. This is especially true of our attitudes toward what we do corporately—as the body of Christ. All the manipulations, the words and acts that are small, mean, and no better than those of any secular group, are regarded with indulgence instead of the aversion our Christian commitment ought to produce.

The plain teaching of the Bible is that while we recognize our own inability to be perfect, we must also face our freedom to choose—in every single instance. We can never say, "I was totally helpless, I couldn't do anything else," without flatly contradicting the Bible. Paul wrote, "No temptation has come your way that is too hard for flesh and blood to bear. But God can be trusted not to allow you to suffer any temptation beyond your powers of endurance. He will see to it that every temptation has a way out, so that it will never be impossible for you to bear it" (1 Cor. 10:13).

He was writing to people who were evidently congratulating themselves on their spiritual attainments, as if they had already reached a state of sinlessness. They were becoming proud, and pride is a dangerous condition, often leading to an ignominious fall. As I read chapter ten of the second letter to Corinth, I get a strong impression that Paul was thinking something like this, "And just in case they turn the argument on me and say, 'Well, if we are going to sin, it's not really our fault—we're incapable of not sinning,' I'd better remind them that sin is not inevitable in any given situation and that God gives strength to those who ask for it."

We don't get much help in avoiding the sin of manipulation within the church, nor for deciding crucial issues without rancor and hard feelings, nor for doing away with power struggles—not because God won't help us, but because we don't ask. We don't commonly admit that these are *sins*. We call them, indulgently, "human nature," or, "Well, you know how people are—we're not perfect." We are far too busy judging those both inside and outside the church to think about our own shortcomings.

The "Respectable" Sins

I have often wondered whether our readiness to condemn drinking, smoking, dancing, and other "sins of the flesh," doesn't blind us to more deadly sins of the spirit. It is certain that in all too many churches a man or woman who smokes or drinks, however moderately, will be judged far more harshly than others who maneuver to control the church board, or bring business pressure to bear on opponents so as to bring them into line.

The point is that these ugly spiritual sins, which are far

too prevalent among us, are often the results of our fears—
our distrust of God. We can't believe that he can manage his
affairs, that the church will be what it should be (or what
we want it to be) without our taking charge. So we try to see
to it that positions of influence and power go to those who
think the same way we do—even if it means a little cloak-
room operating behind the scenes. And when someone labels
such an act for exactly what it is, we come out with the ready
excuse, "Well, of course, when you have an organization
like this, you're bound to have these problems." Problems—
not sins.

I think we're fooling ourselves. My friends and business
acquaintances outside the Christian faith say we are judged
by these very sins. We are judged by the average non-
Christian man or woman who sees nothing very different
about the church from any secular organization. If we are
observed and found wanting by those outside the church,
then what does God think of us? His standards are, we
know, far above those of any human being. I doubt if he
regards our easy acceptance of snobbery and manipulation
with favor.

Facing Reality

If we really intend to be the people of God, then we must
begin to take seriously the matter of living—as individuals
and as a community—by his standards rather than the
world's. This means we must call things by their right
names. Deceit must be deceit, and not "simply making sure
the right point of view is presented." Snobbery must be
acknowledged as such, and not, "He's known as a generous
giver, and that's the sort we want on our church board."
Backbiting and gossip must be seen as sins, and not excused
as, "I'm only telling you this so you can pray about it, my
dear."

As long as we have in our Christian fellowships exactly the same kind of power struggles, half-lies, and undercover warfare that exist outside the church, we are making a lie out of the gospel we preach. A minister once said, with a sigh, that he wished Christians whose business ethics were shabby would at least keep quiet about being Christians since they were such an embarrassment to the rest of us. That is equally true of us as a church. If we aren't living according to a higher standard than the rest of the world, then we have nothing to say to it, and our preaching is nonsense.

We need to be brutally honest with ourselves. It's hard to face these practices we have lived with so long that they have become comfortable, and label them as sins. But that is what they are. And everyone knows it. The scandal of the church in our day is all to often not "the offense of the cross" but the worldliness with which we run our affairs.

A Look at Our Own Motives

Since our tendency to manipulate and control arises most often out of fear rather than a conscious decision to act as if God were helpless, we must examine our own motives and attitudes. Am I standing pat on a certain issue because I really believe it is right, or because I want things to be the way they have always been. Does a new venture displease me because it is inconsistent with the life of the Christian community, or because it is a step outside the safety of a separate and protected church life?

We need to do more than label our efforts to control and manipulate as the sins they are; we must also face the fear that breeds them—an abysmal lack of trust in God. I used to think that it was easy enough to trust God, but terribly difficult to trust other Christians. They frequently made decisions I deplored, expressed sentiments with which I violently disagreed, and failed to see the logic of my arguments. It took a lot of failures on my own part, and some very humbling experiences, for me to begin to realize that God did not need me to mastermind his every move. I discovered he could use people I thought unsuitable. All too often the apparently inept efforts of those whose experience and ability I doubted proved more effective than anything I had envisioned.

In short, I had been guilty of monumental conceit—the assumption that my opinions bore the stamp of divine approval. There are lots of things in my particular church which arouse in me less than enthusiasm; but it's not important that I find everything to my liking. We are a community of widely differing needs and tastes. What is important is that I do—with all my heart—what God has called me to do and trust him to help others play their part well.

—8—

Witnessing—

the Evidence We Give

It's impossible to be really convinced of the merit of a product without telling others. The urge to communicate, to share one's own enthusiasms, is strong in all of us. When it comes to our faith, that urge is reinforced by the biblical command that we should tell what we believe. Yet we're often afraid.

The many Christian organizations which exist in order to teach us how to communicate our faith to the world are prime evidence of the need in this area. One gets the idea that we are afraid to talk about what we believe, about what has happened in our lives, because we don't know how. All we need is a technique, a method, and off we go!

That may be true for some people, and certainly these teaching methods have been helpful to many and the results are evident; but I don't think it's the whole story—or even the main reason for our inability to be effective witnesses for Christ.

What's the Difference?

Most of us are paralyzed as witnesses not because we don't know what to say, but because our lives are no different from most secular people. All around us are non-religious acquaintances who are doing just as well as we are. They are as honest, as truthful, as able to fear affliction, as kind and outgoing as we are—and frequently far more so. We don't say much because we know, with shame, that our conduct is no different from that of the average man or woman.

After all, what do they see of us? When we live so much of our time within the circle of other Christian friends that we have very little to do with those outside the church, the world around us hasn't much to go on. They see us in business, they see us as club members occasionally, as civic workers, or as volunteers in charitable organizations—but not very often. We tend to let most of those projects be carried on by others while we concentrate on the organizational work of the church.

The ghetto view of Christianity which we've been discussing, the belief that the church ought to be a safe haven for Christians produces an anemic kind of witness to the world for two reasons. First, because living cloistered lives engenders an exaggerated fear of what life is like "outside," and second because our witnessing becomes a project, not a genuine outgrowth of our manner of living.

We have already seen that the group which exists in isolation from the world ends up by bringing the world into itself, a microcosm of the secular social structure outside. We place great emphasis on faith, and so we should. Without faith no one comes to Christ in the first place, and without faith it is impossible to live more than a crippled Christian life.

Faith That Works

Everything I read in the Bible about faith, however, tells me that faith produces a certain kind of life. My attitudes, my behavior, everything about me will be influenced or changed radically because of my faith. If it isn't, then the faith doesn't go very deep. Or, as James put it, faith without action is as dead as a body without a soul.

Our faith—always spoken of in the Bible as the antithesis of fear—will determine how we as Christians relate to each other and how we live and work in the world. It is not something we can stir up by ourselves, that's quite impossible, but is given to us by God, when we ask. The reason some of us live such sequestered lives is that we don't give God a chance to give us any faith. He gives the resources we need *when we need them.* If we never get involved in anything outside the walls of our own group, if we never place ourselves where faith is necessary, then no faith will come.

I know that there are experiences which none of us can avoid—we get sick, we lose friends and family by death, we suffer when the economy is low—and God is gracious enough to sustain us when we need it. But there's another kind of faith we also need—the faith to be in close touch with our contemporary culture, in close touch with our neighborhood. That's how we get to know what the thinking of those outside the church is; that's how we get close enough to people who need Christ so we can *be* witnesses. All our talk about faith doesn't mean much if we are seldom in a position to need it.

"You talk as if we could earn God's approval," a woman said during a discussion of Christian living and witnessing. "We are saved by faith, not works, remember, and we have to live by faith."

Several others chimed in at this point, all in support of her position. Bible verses were quoted, and there are certainly many which show clearly that our standing with God is based on faith in Jesus Christ alone and not in anything we have done. These women were all right. But I think they missed the point.

One perceptive woman finally said, "I agree that we live

by faith, as we were saved by faith. But you seem to me to be assuming that 'living by faith' simply means believing certain facts to be true and nothing more—as if what we believe becomes in itself a virtue, and that's all there is to living, just believing certain things. I think the faith called for in the Bible is strong enough to make a difference in the way we live, or it isn't faith at all—only an intellectual assent."

She had the root of the matter in her. We do make an unwarranted leap from "we live by faith," to "and faith is the set of propositions I believe about God, nothing more." It *is* more—faith is what we believe expressed in our lives.

Our Timidity vs. Faith

It seems to me that the emphasis in the evangelical world on a proper faith, while very necessary, has often been stressed at the expense of its essential corollary: how we live because of our faith. We see far too many Christians who don't seem to realize there is a connection between what they believe and what they do. Of course they avoid the obvious "carnal" sins, but tolerate others which Paul listed as being just as bad: hatred, quarreling, jealousy, bad temper, and rivalry. These sins flourish in the very ingrown, protected Christian communities which do the most talking about faith. Our faith, however much we talk about it, is empty.

And our witnessing, as Dr. Donald Williams once pointed out, consists of raiding parties for the purpose of taking captives. We drag them back to the safety of the camp with us (come to our church, we have such a marvelous program) and after awhile they look around, see they are outnumbered, and decide to convert.

Granted, such tactics do make converts, but is that all the New Testament means when we are told, "You are the world's light—it is impossible to hide a town built on the top of a hill. Men do not light a lamp and put it under a bucket. They put it on a lampstand and it gives light for everybody in the house. Let your light shine like that in the sight of men. Let them see the good things you do and praise your Father in heaven" (Matt. 5:14–16).

I cannot believe that Jesus meant by those words nothing more than, "Bring the unsaved into the church so they can see what a fine fellowship you have, and what wonderful times you have together, and how uplifting your church services are." The "good things" men see and for which they praise God must be ordinary good—the good which is plain and understandable to all, not a special kind of piosity observable only in the context of church life.

The call of God is to be faithful to him *in the world*. We must accept the implications of that call—risk, vulnerability, uncertainty—in order to be of any use to him at all. Our natural and very strong desire to be safe needs to be given a proper object. We are safe, kept from any harm to our real selves, even though we face all the threats to temporal life that men everywhere face. I believe the men and women of the early church showed the right response to danger when Peter and John told them of the threats of the Sanhedrin. They immediately began to pray about the opposition of the Jewish rulers and concluded, "And now, O Lord, observe their threats and give thy servants courage to speak thy word fearlessly, while thou dost stretch out thine hand to heal, and cause signs and wonders to be performed in the name of thy holy servant Jesus" (Acts 4:29–30).

Demonstration to the World

They *could* speak the word fearlessly because they were living it. The quality of their fellowship together and their changed lives were being talked about in Jerusalem. They were demonstrating to their world what could happen when

God really gets hold of men and women. How they lived together as a community, as a group of believers, was evidence in itself—and their behavior in the matters of ordinary living was also evidence.

It was that sort of evidence that Paul was speaking of when he said, "If you used to be a thief you must not only give up stealing, but you must learn to make an honest living, so that you may be able to give to those in need. Let there be no more foul language, but good words instead—words suitable for the occasion, which God can use to help other people" (Eph. 4:28–29).

These two kinds of evidence—or two areas of demonstrating the same evidence—are found again and again in the Bible. How we get along with each other, and how we conduct ourselves in the world are the means by which men see what God is doing. Nowhere is there a lesson on witnessing, nor a series of rules for preaching and teaching. It's all lumped together, an inseparable part of everything we are told about living as Christians.

People Giving Evidence

One man I know (and there are many more like him) is a high school teacher whose encouragement and help have influenced hundreds of students. He is an excellent teacher, and his students learn to do their best. They also learn just by seeing the kind of man he is.

A group of young married people get together frequently on a Saturday to work for retired people in the area. They clean houses, do yard work, fix plumbing and broken windows, and take hot meals to their older friends.

Then there is the nurse who gave up a good job in a fine hospital to work as a night nurse in the men's jail ward. She wanted to do something that would help people who are usually not candidates for help. She is no starry-eyed idealist, but a realistic Christian who believes that no corner of the world, even a jail ward, ought to be without someone who knows Christ and cares for people.

Every week at the Hollywood Presbyterian Church a group of men and women who have been trained in the Frank Laubach literacy method meet to teach men and women how to read and write English. They do it because they believe Christ cares about the whole person, and those whom they teach will be able to get better jobs and make better lives for themselves once they can read and write.

The business men and women, the doctors and lawyers, teachers, insurance salesmen, and grocery clerks who are doing something to help others because of their Christian commitment are following Jesus' example. He met people right where they were and took care of their immediate needs. His concern with all of life is shown as well in his teaching. From the Sermon on the Mount to his final command that we preach the gospel everywhere, he talked about how we live every day. Buying, selling, traveling, planting and harvesting, giving dinner parties, and being entertained—these are, he said, the activities which demonstrate what we are. How we handle material things and how we treat each other in the everyday affairs of life show what we believe.

. . . but Is It "Orthodox"?

His teaching was considered revolutionary, and so was his life. He certainly broke all the rules and ignored the customs which marked Israel's religious leaders. They—the Pharisees and scribes, the Sadducees and Herodians—were the segregationists of their day. They believed and taught that the Gentiles were so unclean that their touch, or even their shadow, contaminated the Jew. Jesus, to their horror, went right through the land of the Samaritans, a people of mixed Jewish and Gentile blood and therefore despised. Not only that, but he spent time in the Decapolis across the Jordan, also a partly Gentile area.

Even if he had kept within the boundries of "the land," his behavior would have offended these religious separatists, for they prided themselves on being the theological intelligentsia. Their study of the law and the countless hedges, restrictions, and amplifications built up around it, as well as their observance of minute ritual customs, were the demonstrations of their piety. They believed that even other Jews, who kept all the religious observances and followed the law of Moses but who were not learned in the fine points of the law, were inferior, "accursed."

If we want a biblical example for our segregated Christian communities, we must look at the Jewish nation as it was in Jesus' day. The Jews were careful to have nothing to do with Gentiles, or those of mixed blood. The students of the law and religious leaders had nothing to do with ordinary people. Jewish society had come a long way from the twelve tribes of nomads who had settled the Promised Land. It had become structured in a way that walled groups off. It was this society that Jesus cut across, both with his teaching and his life-style.

He had dinner with all the wrong people, the socially unacceptable. He chose ordinary men as disciples, not scholars. He ignored the regulations guarding the sanctity of the Sabbath, and his stories not only showed how unbiblical the traditions had become but did it with biting humor which made the religionists furious.

"When you give a luncheon or a dinner party," he said, "don't invite your friends or your brothers or relations or wealthy neighbors, for the chances are they will invite you back, and you will be fully repaid. No, when you give a party, invite the poor, the lame, the crippled and the blind . . ." (Luke 14:12–14).

When we live exclusively in our Christian societies, then, having very little to do with those outside, we are in the tradition of the religionists of Israel. Jesus' call is to something entirely different. We must go, as he did, out among the undistinguished, unreligious, unacceptable people of the world.

Not Just Another Oddball

And that going has to be real—not merely an appearance, not merely to give a prepared talk on what Christ can do, and then hurry back to the safety of the group. Our witnessing must arise naturally out of the situations we find ourselves in along with everyone else. I think they'll listen when they see genuine honesty and concern and a love which expresses itself in doing, not merely saying. And they have to see these things close up—that means getting next to those outside the faith in real friendship. They must really *know* *us* and we must know them—not as objects of our zeal for witnessing, but as those we love for themselves.

My daughter, Donna, worked for a large firm in Southern California some years ago. This area seems to be the breeding place for innumerable off-beat religions, and several of her colleagues belonged to such groups. Many of them were prone to hold forth on their convictions—to the tolerant amusement of their hearers. Most of the people in the department, average secular folk, joked about the oddballs in their midst. No one took them seriously.

Not long after Donna had gone to work there, one of her more spiritual friends asked her gravely if she had given her witness as a Christian. Donna looked at her thoughtfully and replied, "If you mean have I given a little canned testimony, no. They listen to all kinds of people sound off and if I did the same thing they'd simply put me down as another nut."

She had not been there long, however, before everyone seemed to know she was a Christian. Not because she handed out pious little sayings, but because in her everyday conversation and manner of working her faith became apparent. People asked questions and she had opportunities to talk with them about her faith. The people who asked, however, were people with whom she had developed a friendship. There was a relationship there out of which something new could come, the witness was not simply flung out like a television commercial.

There Are No Shortcuts

Could it be that our fear of witnessing arises out of the fact that we are trying to take a shortcut and talk to people without having first established any relationship at all? It's difficult to take any conversation beyond the shallows when two strangers meet—the things we say are polite and exploratory until we find common ground and can go on to know one another better.

We are afraid of witnessing because we think we don't speak well enough, or can't quote Bible verses, or haven't the assurance of a public speaker. But all those handicaps become unimportant when we are talking to someone we know well enough to be comfortable with. It isn't just that *we* need to be comfortable in order to talk about our faith, it's that the other person needs to be comfortable.

There will always be risks in witnessing. But they will not be the ones we have feared the most—of being laughed at or rejected or received with hostility. They will simply be the risks we incur when we get close enough to people to let them into our lives. We may be hurt, we will certainly be inconvenienced and the neat pattern of our lives will be disturbed. There may be a certain timidity to overcome in making ourselves so vulnerable to others but that's a fear which quickly fades as we begin to enjoy the adventure of real life in the real world.

—9—

Freedom from Fear

Fear keeps us from being happy even when circumstances ought to make us happy. How can we enjoy anything when we're constantly haunted by the specter of imminent disaster? Grief and pain are limited. They exist because of specific situations; but fear casts a pall over everything.

Fear not only destroys all happiness, it makes us ineffective as Christians, as we have seen. The locked-in Christian, like the locked-in church, is neither happy nor effective. There is every reason to face our fears instead of cowering under them. The little boy in the poem who was terrified of "seein' things at night" only saw those goblins in the dark. Our fears are the same way—they live in the dark, and when we turn on them and drag them out into the light they often turn out to be rather insubstantial.

I am convinced that most of the problems that exist in the ghetto church—the preoccupation with the appearance, snobbishness, provincialism and the judgemental spirit that prevail in such an atmosphere—make for unhappy Christians. There's no freedom, no joy, in such a climate. We'd all be better off if we accepted the risks that go with venturing out into our world than we are huddled together in rigid little bundles. Most of our apprehensions would disappear as goblins disappear when the light is turned on.

Our fear of witnessing is seen to be a shadow with no substance at all when we realize that witnessing is simply the evidence of our total lives for Christ, not a special technique we must master. It is what we are, as well as what we say and it takes place every day, as we live our ordinary lives.

A class of seminary students was once asked by the professor to tell what single influence brought each one to Christ. Some said a particular sermon moved them to a decision; a few mentioned having heard a personal testimony which hit home; but the greater portion of the class members said it was the influence of someone well known—a brother, sister, parent, or friend. I believe that is how most of us arrive at our faith. We are moved, imperceptibly and by degrees, by the evidence of those around us. And, in turn, we are most effective as Christians in the matters of everyday living.

The Goblin of Failure

What we are and how we react in ordinary circumstances is a more convincing demonstration of our faith than what we say when we are on stage, so to speak, and conscious of being observed. But we have to get close enough to people so they can see beneath the surface, just as we must know them and care for them as friends rather than objects of our benevolence. Simply saying "hello" with a smile to those we work with, or chatting over a coffee break or luncheon isn't enough. Getting to know someone means having dinner parties together, letting acquaintance ripen into friendship, caring about the things that matter to each other.

It means being inconvenienced, being available when one would rather have time to oneself, listening to other people's problems, and sharing one's own. It means abandoning the mask of the glossy, always happy, never frustrated Christian and letting one's real self be known.

When we do that, we banish the goblin of the fear of failure and rejection. We discover that it's not our failure to be always right that defeats our witness, it's our pretense that we are. There is a great difference between those who are following Christ with all they have in them but stumble from time to time and those who are putting up a great show of always being spiritually on top. From all I have seen, and from the frank comments I've heard by those outside the church, any average non-Christian can tell the difference.

What the world is looking for is some evidence of reality and strength beyond ourselves in our lives. I believe there are people all around us who are hungry for reality and looking for the truth, and that they will respond when they see it in us. Not a phony appearance of spirituality, but the genuineness of commitment to Christ will be convincing. And that means being able to say, "That was wrong, and I'm sorry. With God's help I intend to do better."

When we are able to admit failure, we discover that we can get up again and go on. Acknowledging our failures and then plunging right in again frees us from another fear—the fear of being seen as we are, not as the "perfect Christian." For many of us discovering that we are accepted with all our imperfections and faults is a liberating experience almost like that of conversion. I know it was so for me.

Having been brought up, as we all have, in a performance-oriented culture so that I was always fearful that any failure on my part would cast me into outer darkness, I was always a little tense. I didn't give up the effort to project an image of perfection out of virtue, or a sudden access of spirituality, simply out of fatigue. I got tired of being on edge all the time. I remember very well the evening my final deliverance came—and I do hope this story will not seem offensive or unchristian to the more pious readers; to most I think it will awaken an echo in their own hearts.

Freedom to Be Ourselves

At a party given by the Sunday school class to which I belong the evening's program was concluded by a brief talk by one of the ministers on our staff. I cannot remember anything of his talk except the final sentence: "Now I want you to turn your chairs and get into small groups of four or five and then each one of you tell the others what new blessing or insight into God's plan you have had today." We did as we were told and I found myself in a group I knew well, which may account for what happened. One person after another told about the thoughts they had had while driving to work or doing the dishes and what great spiritual truths had come to them. I grew more and more depressed. Finally it was my turn and I was too disgruntled and tired to say more than, "Well, I've had a hell of a day and I don't want another one like it for a long time!"

I can't remember much about the reaction of the group, except that most of them laughed indulgently—but my own reaction was explosive. I thought, "My goodness, for the first time in my life I have said *exactly* how I feel without tidying it up a little to impress my Christian friends. I feel wonderful!"

Now I don't mean that we should make it a point to be as blunt and tactless as possible. Tact is still a wonderful smoother of the social waters. But I do mean that when we drop the pretense that we are always up, always spiritually blooming, we find a new freedom. We find that others do accept us as we are, perhaps even with a kind of relief as they themselves are encouraged to be more honest. Most of us, free of the necessity to appear to be perfect at all times, find our own relaxed attitude very encouraging to others.

We must be prepared for a certain resistance from some people, however. One woman said as a group of us were talking in this vein, "I think you're all on the wrong track. You sound as if we should just let down and be no better than everyone else. Aren't Christians supposed to be always loving and kind and forgiving? We're supposed to be separated from the world, and that means we have to be different." The discussion that followed got fairly intense at times and went all the way from the original topic—being honest about ourselves—to the question of how much we could be involved in the world without compromising our Christian morality and ethics.

My conviction about the first issue—whether or not being honest about our feelings and about where we are spiritually is simply giving up the effort to follow Christ—is that our only hope is to be honest. After all, everyone outside the faith is involved to some degree in pretense. Real transparency is something only we Christians can afford; to the rest of the world, it's too dangerous. Concealment and the projection of an image which is acceptable to others is the way society at large functions. Being different from the world means, among other things, being free to be honest about oneself. We are most free, most truly ourselves and at the same time truly Christ's when we come out from behind the protective masks most of us wear. When we are free to admit our failures, free to admit the real state of matters in our lives, we are, in actual fact, separating ourselves from the world. And that brings us to the second question.

Separated . . . How?

We've said a great deal about the necessity of our being Christ's men and women in the world, and I think we have to consider seriously just how we can do that and still maintain a firm stance as Christians. In what way are we separated from the world? There are those who quote 2 Corinthians 6:14 as their reason for living lives almost completely apart from the world: "Be ye not unequally yoked together with unbelievers; for what fellowship hath righteousness with unrighteousness? and what concord hath Christ with Belial?" (kjv).

The Phillips version puts the opening phrase this way: "Don't link up with unbelievers and try to work with them"; *The New English Bible* says, "Do not unite yourselves with unbelievers; they are no fit mates for you."

The words sound very exclusive, a direct contradiction to everything I've said about giving up the safety of the segregated life.

It must be considered in the light of the entire Bible, however, especially the New Testament which was written by—and for the church as the body of Christ. No part of Scripture can be properly understood apart from the whole, and whenever any group has emphasized one aspect of its teaching at the expense of others the result has been either a wildly unbalanced approach to life or an outright heresy.

With that in mind we may ask what Paul meant by his advice and how does it fit with the entirety of biblical teaching? For instance, how does it fit with Jesus' prayer for his disciples recorded in John 17:15—"I am not praying that you will take them out of the world but that you will keep them from the evil one."

. . . in our Needy World . . .

The world is as much the subject of the entire prayer as the disciples (and us). It is the created world (v. 5), the world in which he leaves his disciples (v. 11), and though he prays for the disciples specifically rather than the world, (v. 9), it is the world to which he was sent and to which we also are sent (vv. 18–19), and finally it is the world that may believe that God did indeed send his Son when it sees the disciples of Christ living in him.

The world which Jesus said hated his followers as it had hated him is where we are to live and be witnesses for him. The witness, according to the prayer, consists of the evidence of our lives both verbally and by what we are by being united to Christ. The relationship between Christ and the Father is continually mentioned as a pattern for the relationship between his church and Christ. It would seem logical, then, to look at Christ's relationship with the world as our pattern for our relationship to the world.

Reading the Gospels shows us Jesus traveling throughout his country with his small group of followers, teaching, preaching, evidently making some special friends—Mary, Martha and Lazarus, for instance. Traveling teachers of the law were not unusual in Israel, but it was Jesus himself who was so startling, it was what he was that either amazed or confounded those who met him. He went to dinner parties with quite ordinary people, even socially unacceptable people, which infuriated the religionists; he healed all who asked him for healing and he made no efforts to get any special hearing with the "best" people. He was concerned over the physical needs of people—the feeding of the multitude and his numerous miraculous healings attest to that—but at the same time pointed out that material or physical benefits are less important than being spiritually whole.

We see Jesus talking to people on their own level, using stories about everyday life they could readily understand, always responding to the immediate need, showing no social discrimination at all, and so surrounded by hordes of people that occasionally he went away quietly to pray by himself, but always returning to the crowd. He was certainly, in the physical sense, "with them." He was with them in his concern for them as total beings, spiritual as well as physical; but he was never "of them."

His point of view was from the Father, not from men, and

the hostility and tension he evoked from some quarters was because of that point of view. When he acted in a way that shocked the religious sensibilities of the Pharisees, it was the point of view behind the act, so opposed to theirs, which was at stake.

It seems to me, therefore, that our position in the world should be, as far as we have it in us, like his. We ought to be concerned about those around us—their physical needs, their psychological needs, their whole selves—not just their souls. That which separates us from the world ought to be our point of view and our goals, and any difference in life style should come from that, not from artificially created distinctions. We go through life with a different goal from those who are not Christians—we are set on pleasing God, with living according to his will. The difference between us and the average secular person will be more profound, because our motives are different, than the superficial differences Christian groups have often set up as marks of spirituality.

Risk Is Inevitable

The risks we take by living this way will also be more perilous than those of the Christian whose chief contacts in his world are confined to business or a profession, and the usual formal "witnessing." They only risk some social displeasure if their testimonies are not well received, some ridicule or resentment.

Living and moving in the secular world according to Christ's teaching, however—once we take him seriously— is hazardous indeed. It means being absolutely honest in everything, even if it is to our own disadvantage. There is no promise in the New Testament, by the way, that our own honesty will be met by equal honesty from others. We may be cheated.

If we make a serious attempt to follow New Testament

teaching, our relationships with the most casual acquaintances and business colleagues will be invested with all the concern and thoughtfulness and honesty and love of which we are capable. That makes us vulnerable, and there is no guarantee that we won't get hurt. In fact, living as a Christian in this world is like going into a battle without visible armor and weapons. Perhaps Paul was thinking of this very fact when he advised the Ephesians to be strong not in themselves but in the Lord.

But We Do Have Armor

The armor he recommended is hardly that which is considered essential for survival in this competitive and pragmatic world: truth, instead of a clever sales pitch; righteousness instead of power to manipulate; the gospel of peace instead of divisiveness; salvation rather than doing the competition in, the sword of the Spirit, not political or economic clout; and finally, our only purely defensive weapon—faith rather than influential friends in high places.

In spite of the fact that we talk about them a lot, I have a suspicion that we are prone to regard these spiritual resources as rather fragile defenses against an obviously ruthless social structure. We tend to keep them tucked away in a corner of our thinking, labeled, "Use when all else fails." They *are* fragile if we are thinking in terms of the common and very possible disasters I've mentioned—being hurt by those to whom we offer friendship and love, being swindled by people less honest than we are, or being ridiculed because our scruples make us seem simple. But they are, in fact, very strong and our only defense against any hurt to our real selves.

I believe that much of our exclusiveness as Christians, the reason we hide within our cozy little groups is due to our reluctance to accept the element of risk in the Christian life and our wish-theology (and that is what it is) that spirituality somehow entitles us to safety from injury to our bodies, our pocketbooks and our sensitivities. We would rather read and memorize all the comforting, reassuring passages in the Bible than those in which Jesus tells us very plainly what our risks will be and what our attitude is to be: "Never be afraid of those who can kill the body but are powerless to kill the soul!" Surely it is significant that Jesus' final talk with his small band of disciples the night of his betrayal, from which we love to quote his comforting words about the many mansions in the Father's house, concludes with these: "You will find trouble in the world—but, never lose heart, I have conquered the world!"

He conquered it, of course, by the very means we are so reluctant to use as our only weapons, and his final triumph was on the cross. Only when we do accept the risk and the danger inherent in the Christian life will we be strong enough to give up using the church as a sanctuary from the world and accept it for what it was meant to be—the family of God, the home *from which we go forth* to be Christ's men and women in the world.

The Freedom of Risk

There is an unexpected freedom which comes as a result of accepting the implications of vulnerability and the risk of being hurt which are part of the gospel—an exhilarating freedom from fear. It sounds unlikely, but it is so. Instead of saying to ourselves, "Well, all right, if I must take chances and possibly suffer for my faith, I will," with a kind of subdued resignation, we discover that the possibility of getting hurt isn't as frightening as it was.

Perhaps it is akin to the joy of battle which comes when one is totally committed to the struggle; or it may be that God will not give us the reassurance and strength we need until we are in a position to use it. Certainly as long as we are huddled together behind the walls of the church we're in no danger from the world and therefore in no need of anything from God—except a strong shove outward.

We need to remind ourselves that when Jesus talked about himself as the shepherd and his followers as sheep, he said, "He calls his own sheep by name and leads them *out of the fold*, and when he has driven all his own flock outside, he goes in front of them himself, and the sheep follow him because they know his voice." If, in the church, his voice occasionally seems lost in the hubbub of committee meetings, planning sessions, voices of dissent and even testimonies, we may hear it again speaking to us from outside—out there in the world he came to save.

Yes, I do believe Jesus came to deliver us from fear as well as from the power of Satan. He did not promise us a safe life, away from all possible risk and harm, but he did promise us nothing could really touch our real selves as long as we are in him. We may, as Paul said, be knocked down but we are never knocked out!

We may be scared from time to time, but we do not need to be paralyzed by fear. After all, we know where we're going and we know we are loved by God. When we need them, there are countless words of reassurance to be found in the Bible. We read them and they resound in our minds. Perhaps the words which will sound the loudest are those of Jesus: "Fear not . . . fear not . . . fear not."